WILLS, PROBATE AND ADMINISTRATION

Revision WorkBook

Editor: Alison Baxter BA (Oxon)

HLT Publications

HLT PUBLICATIONS
200 Greyhound Road, London W14 9RY

ISBN 1 85352 898 6

British Library Cataloguing-in-Publication.

A CIP Catalogue record for this book is available from the British Library.

Printed and bound in Great Britain.

CONTENTS

ACKNOWLEDGEMENT

Some questions used are taken or adapted from past Solicitors' Final Examination papers set by the Law Society and our thanks are extended to the Law Society for their kind permission to use and publish the questions.

Caveat

The answers given are not approved or sanctioned by the Law Society and are entirely our responsibility.

They are not intended as 'Model Answers', but rather as Suggested Solutions.

The answers have two fundamental purposes, namely:

a) To provide a detailed example of a suggested solution to an examination question, and

b) To assist students with their research into the subject and to further their understanding and appreciation of the subject.

INTRODUCTION

This Revision WorkBook is aimed to be of help to those studying the Law Society's Final Examination on wills, probate and administration. Students will hopefully find it useful not only at examination time but also as a helpful summary of and introduction to the subject when studying it for the first time.

The WorkBook has been designed specifically to address common problems suffered by students when studying any legal subject.

a) *Acquisition of knowledge*

   This is achieved by individual work - attending lectures and reading the relevant materials. The WorkBook is not intended to be a substitute for these materials. However, the 'key points' section will help students to direct their study to the important areas within each topic.

b) *Applying the knowledge to the question*

   This is, perhaps, the most common problem of all. The WorkBook includes examination questions and answers covering many possible question variations within each topic. All such 'model answers' are of a length which a student could reasonably be expected to produce under the time restraints of an examination.

[illegible] STUDY WILLS, PROBATE AND ADMINISTRATION

[illegible] wills, probate and administration. Students will know that Wills, Probate and Administration (WPA) is one of the nine compulsory subjects which are examined in the Law Society's Final Examination. In WPA as in the other subjects, the course emphasises on the absorption of a lot of material and its practical application, [illegible] a will. The subject [illegible] divides itself into two parts – pre-death matters and post-death matters – although [illegible] tax [illegible] parts.

[illegible] lectures and [illegible] materials. [illegible] key points [illegible]

[illegible]

[illegible] examination questions, and answers [illegible] within each topic. [illegible] answers [illegible] reasonably be expected to produce [illegible]

HOW TO STUDY WILLS, PROBATE AND ADMINISTRATION

Wills, probate and administration (WPA) is one of the nine compulsory subjects which are examined in the Law Society's Final Examination. In WPA as in the other subjects, the course emphasis is on the absorption of a lot of material and its practical application; the latter may constitute advising a client or drafting a will. The subject, and often the examination, divides itself into two parts - pre-death matters and post-death matters - although certain topics, such as tax, fall into both parts.

REVISION AND EXAMINATION TECHNIQUE

Whole books have been written on how to study and this brief note makes no pretence at being an infallible guide. In any case, skill in revision and examination techniques is an art best acquired by actual practice.

The more you study, the more you devise your own short cuts for efficient preparation for exams. Unfortunately, it is only when you actually sit the examination that you can see whether your particular method of revision is successful. If it is not, it is an expensive and frustrating way to find out.

While it is true that examination techniques are best learned actually sitting examinations, it is not necessary to wait until the real thing. 'Mock' examinations, tackled under realistic conditions, can be very helpful. Revision aids like this Workbook, not only give some idea of potential questions and possible solutions, but can be used most efficiently by the student as a form of examination rehearsal. For example, select a question and, without looking at the skeleton answer, write out your own. Compare it with the skeleton answer in the Workbook and if you appear to be working along the right lines, then proceed to write a full solution - preferably under simulated examination conditions. Once you have completed your own solution you can see how it tallies with that given in the Workbook.

Remember, none of the solutions given is represented as the 'only' solution, nor need the exact sequence be the same - the main aim is to give you guidance as to a possible way of tackling the question and as to presentation of your answer.

Most people who have succeeded in examinations have times when they think: 'If only I had known then, what I know now, I could have done even better.' For that reason it is often helpful to read other people's suggestions and hints for easier revision and any tips they may have for actually sitting the examination - such advice is often prompted by bitter experience!

Often a large number of such recommendations en masse are rather overwhelming. Indeed, some may actually contradict each other. The secret is to use only that advice which applies to you personally and which you think will fit in with your chosen methods of study.

However, remember that recognizing that what is effective is a personal matter does not mean there are no ground rules at all. The most important thing to remember is that in studying for an exam your success (or lack of it) will be entirely due to your own efforts. The secret of success is to realise at an early stage that it is necessary to create an efficient pattern of study which suits your own character and with which you will feel comfortable.

The short list of Do's and Dont's below attempts to set out some suggestions which it is hoped most students will find of practical use in planning their revision and tackling examinations.

Do's

a) *Planning ahead*

Plan ahead and make your plans increasingly detailed as you approach the examination date.

Allocate enough time for each topic to be studied. It is better to devise a realistic timetable, to which you have a reasonable chance of keeping, rather than a wildly optimistic schedule which you will abandon at the first opportunity.

b) *Self-discipline*

Exercise constant self-discipline, especially if studying at home.

c) *Self-testing*

Constantly test yourself during your course of study, especially once revision starts, both orally and in writing.

d) *Past exam papers*

Familiarise yourself with past examination papers; and try at least one 'mock examination' well before the date of the real thing.

e) *Exam paper instruction*

Read the instructions at the examination carefully. While any last minute changes are unlikely - such as the introduction of a compulsory question - it has been known to happen.

f) *Exam questions*

Read the questions carefully. Analyse problem questions - work out what the examiner wants. Plan your answer before you start to write.

g) *Mark allocations*

Note mark allocations on the question paper. It is pointless to spend an excessive amount of time in producing a perfect answer to a part of a problem that carries only a tiny percentage of the marks.

Don'ts

a) *Completing the syllabus*

Don't finish the syllabus too early - constant revision of the same topic leads to stagnation - but don't leave revision so late that you have to 'cram'.

If you are the sort of person who works better to a deadline - make it a realistic one!

b) *Learning by rote*

Don't try to learn by rote. In particular, don't try to reproduce model answers by heart. Learn to express the basic concepts in your own words.

c) *Answering the right question*

Don't answer the question you expect to see! By all means 'problem-spot' before examinations by going over old exam papers but make sure that what the examiner is asking for really does match what you are preparing to write about.

d) *Keeping calm*

DON'T PANIC!

TABLE OF CASES

TABLE OF STATUTES

PART ONE
PRE-DEATH

1 INTESTACY

1.1 Introduction

A person dies intestate if he has either made no effective will (total intestacy) or if his will fails to deal with the whole of his estate - if there is no effective provision for the residue of the estate (partial intestacy).

1.2 Key points

Administration of Estates Act 1925 (AEA) s33 provides that personal representatives (PRs) hold property undisposed of by will on 'statutory trusts for sale' with power to postpone sale for as long as they think fit.

The statutory trusts provide that the property should be dealt with as follows:

a) to pay funeral and testamentary expenses, debts, liabilities and administration expenses; *and*

b) then to set aside a fund to pay the pecuniary legacies; *and*

c) then to distribute any remainder among the beneficiaries entitled on intestacy.

NB:

By s33(7), s33 is subject to provisions contained in the will. Thus, if undisposed of property is subject to an express trust for sale under the will then those terms will apply and those of the statutory trusts will not.

Reversionary interests must not be sold until they fall into possession unless a special reason exists to do so (eg to pay debts).

Personal chattels should not be sold unless there is a special reason to do so.

Who takes what?

a) *Spouse* (does not include one who is divorced or judicially separated)

   i) If intestate leaves issue, spouse takes:

      - 'personal chattels' (as defined by AEA s55(1)(x)) absolutely; *and*
      - £75,000 free of tax and costs, plus interest at 6 per cent from death until payment; *and*
      - a life interest in half of the residue.

   ii) If intestate leaves no issue but either a parent of the whole blood or a brother or sister of the whole blood or issue of such, spouse takes:

- 'personal chattels' (as above) absolutely; *and*
- £125,000 free of tax and costs, plus interest at 6 per cent from death until payment; *and*
- half of the residue absolutely.

iii) If intestate leaves none of the above, spouse takes the whole estate absolutely.

b) *Special rules concerning the spouse - rights*

Spouse can elect to:

i) Redeem the life interest (in (a)(iii) above) for a lump sum out of capital.

The spouse must give written notice to the PRs within 12 months of the grant of their wish to capitalise the life interest. (If the spouse is the sole PR, notice must be given to the Senior Registrar of the Family Division.)

The PRs must obtain a valuation unless all the other beneficiaries are of full age and capacity, in which case they can agree one amongst themselves. The exercise of this right does not qualify as a transfer for IHT purposes (see chapter 9).

ii) Take the matrimonial home (or the deceased's share of it) as part of their absolute (and capitalised, if relevant) interest.

'Matrimonial Home' is any dwelling house in which the spouse was resident at the time of the intestate's death - Intestates' Estates Act 1952 (IEA).

Spouse must given written notice to the PRs within 12 months of the grant. (The PRs must not sell within that 12 months without the written consent of the spouse unless compelled to do so. If they do so, however, the spouse has no rights against the purchaser.)

The house is valued at the date at which it is appropriated to the spouse (and thus it is best to elect as soon as possible).

NB:

- If the property is held as joint tenants it will pass outside intestacy.
- The right is not available for leasehold interests where the lease is due to end within two years of the intestate's death.
- If the spouse is a PR:

  if sole PR, must apply to court for consent *or* obtain consent of all other beneficiaries (if of full age) *or* get another PR appointed;

  if not, spouse can exercise the right despite the rule that a trustee should not purchase trust property.

- If the house is used for non-domestic purposes or is held with agricultural land, the consent of the court is necessary.
- AEA s41 could be used to achieve the same result. Under this provision, any person entitled on intestacy can agree with the PRs to take any assets not specifically disposed of elsewhere in satisfaction of their entitlement.

c) *Special rules concerning spouse - hotchpot*

On partial intestacy, the spouse must account for any benefits under the will apart from personal chattels, as against their absolute interest.

d) *Special rules concerning spouse - Law of Property Act 1925 (LPA) s184*

Under s184, where no evidence exists as to the order of death of persons, they are presumed to have died in order of seniority for the purposes of succession to property.

However, the IEA provides that s184 does not apply between husband and wife if the elder dies wholly or partially intestate. In this case, the property passing under the intestacy of the elder devolves as though the younger did not survive (ie if the elder dies intestate, the younger is presumed to predecease).

Wills often include survivorship clauses which avoid the operation of s184 (see chapter 2).

e) *Other beneficiaries*

i) Subject to the spouses rights, the estate goes to the intestate's:

- issue on 'statutory trusts'; but if none to
- parents equally (if both alive); but if none to
- brother and sisters of the whole blood (or their issue per stirpes) on 'statutory trusts'.

ii) If neither spouse nor any beneficiary mentioned in (i) above exist, then to:

- brothers and sisters of the half blood on 'statutory trusts'; but if none to
- uncles and aunts of the half blood on 'statutory trusts'; but if none
- bona vacantia.

f) *Statutory trusts*

'Statutory trusts' means:

- equally for all members of the class alive or en ventre sa mére of the intestate's death; *and*
- who attains 18 or marries earlier.

If an infant fails to attain 18 or marry earlier, the intestate's estate will be redistributed to those who would have been entitled at the date of the intestate's death as if the infant had never existed. If some beneficiaries (over 18) have died since the intestate's death, their share goes to their estate.

Issue of members who predecease the intestate take per stirpes their parent's share provided they attain 18 or marry earlier.

g) *Hotchpot*

Advancement (payment or settlement on the marriage of the child or to establish the child in life) made inter vivos by the deceased to the child must be brought into account by the child (or issue if the child predeceases) in determining the child's share on intestacy. This is subject to express or implied contrary intention. The advancement is valued as at the intestate's death.

Gifts by will by the deceased to issue must be brought into account on partial intestacy. As a result, any issue of the testator who takes on partial intestacy must bring into account everything taken under the will by his branch of the family.

This, too, is subject to contrary intention and the gift is valued as at the intestate's death.

h) *Special rules re children*

On intestacy, no distinction is made between people whose parents are or were married to each other and people whose parents are not or were not.

(A person whose parents were not married to each other at the time of his birth are presumed not to have been survived by the father or relations on the father's side.)

Adopted children are related to their adoptive parents.

Legitimated children are deemed both legitimate and can take an interest on intestacy.

2 THE WILL

2.1 Introduction

There are many reasons why a person is well advised to make a will directing what is to happen to his property after his death. If he does not, the intestacy provisions in chapter 1 will apply. A will can take many forms, but for it to be valid certain requirements must be complied with.

2.2 Key points

a) *Reasons for making a will*

- i) Direct how to dispose of the estate, rather than rely on intestacy rules.
- ii) Positive demonstration of generosity.
- iii) Exercise a choice of executors and make administration more convenient.
- iv) Extend the statutory powers of executors.
- v) Appoint testamentary guardians.
- vi) Tax considerations (see chapter 9).
- vii) Peace of mind.
- viii) Burial considerations and arrangements.

b) *Duty of the solicitors*

The solicitor must ensure:

- i) That the will is valid - the testator must have capacity, intention and must observe Wills Act 1837 (WA) s9 (see post).
- ii) That it accurately expresses the testator's wishes.

c) *Information necessary to take instructions*

- i) Is there an existing will? Has it been revoked or changed by codicil(s)?
- ii) Testator's family and dependants.
- iii) What are their needs and resources?

  (NB: a possible claim under IPFDA - see chapter 3 - and consider putting a statement with the will explaining why property is not being left to possible claimants.)

iv) Nature and composition of the estate

Need an idea of size for tax purposes, and of property eligible for IHT reliefs (see chapter 9).

Consider types of property not passing by will and explain effect of this to client - joint property (cannot sever by will); nominated property (cannot revoke by will); insurance policies in trust for others (cannot leave it under the will); pensions.

v) Lifetime transfers

Consider inter vivos tax planning (see chapter 9).

vi) Review

Provisions of a will should be reviewed regularly, especially if Revenue Law of the testator's circumstances change.

d) *Preparation of the will*

i) Age - the testator must be over 18.

ii) Mental capacity - the testator must understand:

- nature and effect of making a will; *and*
- extent of his property; *and*
- moral claims he should consider.

In general, the propounder of the will must prove that the testator had capacity, on a balance of probabilities, when the will was executed (signed and witnessed) unless:

- if the will appears rational, capacity is presumed;
- if the testator generally lacked mental capacity, a lack of capacity will be presumed unless it can be shown that the testator recovered capacity at the time of execution.

If there is any doubt as to capacity, medical advice should be taken. A doctor should attest, if possible, and a full attendance note should be taken.

iii) Intention (at the time of execution)

- General intention - the testator must intend to make a will; *and*
- Specific intention - the testator must intend to make the will in question (he must know and approve its contents).

Intention is presumed from the fact that the testator had capacity and executed the will. The presumption can be rebutted by proving:

- the testator was induced by force or fear or fraud; *or*
- the testator was subjected to undue influence; *or*

- part of the will was included by mistake. This is possible if:

  the testator executes the wrong document; *or*

  the testator includes words he does not know and approve.

Exceptions to the presumption:

- The testator is blind or illiterate or the will is signed by someone else on his behalf. In this case, intention must be proved. (The will should be read to the testator in the presence of witnesses and a different attestation clause should be used.)

- There are suspicions circumstances (eg the will substantially benefits the person who prepares it. This is a question of fact. If the benefit is substantial, suggest that the client takes independent advice.) The propounder must remove the suspicion.

Any part of the will which is not intended will not be admitted to probate.

iv) Formalities (attesting the will)

Wills Act 1837 s9 - for a will to be valid, it must be:

- in writing and signed by the testator or by someone in his presence and at his direction; *and*

- it must appear that the testator intended by his signature to give effect to the will; *and*

- the signature must be made or acknowledged by the testator in the presence of two or more witnesses present at the same time; *and*

- each witness must either:

  attest and sign the will; *or*

  acknowledge his signature

  in the presence of the testator (but not necessarily in the presence of the other witness(es)).

Procedure

If the testator signs or acknowledges his own signature, two witnesses must be present (physically and mentally) when he does so. The witnesses must then sign or acknowledge their signatures in the presence (physical and mental) of the testator.

If someone signs for the testator, he must sign in the testator's presence and at his direction, and in the presence of the witnesses. The witnesses must then sign or acknowledge their signatures as above.

Attestation clauses

An attestation clause is not necessary, but is advisable because if one is used the presumption of due execution is raised. If such a clause is not used, an affidavit of due execution will be required in order to admit the will to probate.

v) *Witnesses*

Witnesses must be capable of physical and mental presence.

Wills Act 1837 s15 - if a will is witnessed by a person who (or whose spouse) obtains a benefit under the will, the benefit is lost. However, this is subject to an exception under the Wills Act 1968: if, after disregarding the signatures of the beneficiary-witness(es), the will has still been validly executed (ie there are at least two other witnesses who are not beneficiaries or spouses of beneficiaries), then s15 does not apply and the gifts are still valid.

vi) Incorporation of other documents

Unexecuted documents

An unexecuted document will become part of a will (by the doctrine of incorporation) if:

- it is in existence at the date of the will; *and*
- it is referred to in the will as already in existence; *and*
- it is clearly identified or identifiable from the will.

If there is a subsequent codicil, the unexecuted document will be incorporated if:

- it is in existence at the date of codicil (but not necessarily at the date of the will);
- it is referred to as already in existence by either the will or the codicil; *and*
- it can be clearly identified from either the will or the codicil.

An incorporated document is public.

Codicils (executed documents)

The execution of a codicil republishes the will, provided that there is an indication of intention to do so. (Any reference to the will is sufficient intention.) The result is that the will takes effect as if it were executed at the date of the codicil.

e) *Types of legacies*

i) Specific (eg my antique vase)

A specific legacy will often be preceded by the word 'my'. If the item is not owned by the testator at death, the gift will fail. (The testator should, therefore, be asked what he wants to happen in this event. A substitutional gift is possible.)

If the testator leaves specific property to be shared between more than one beneficiary, he should specify how the decision about the division is to be made.

ii) General (eg 100 shares in ICI)

If the testator does not own the property at death, the personal representatives must purchase it.

iii) Demonstrative (eg £100 to be paid out of my Halifax building society account)

A demonstrative legacy is a general legacy payable out of a particular fund or particular property. It remains payable even if the fund or property is not in existence at the testator's death. If the testator does not wish this to happen, the gift should be worded as conditional on the existence of the fund or property.

iv) Pecuniary (eg £100)

A pecuniary legacy is a gift of money. A pecuniary legacy will also be either specific, general or demonstrative.

v) Residuary

The residuary legacy is what is left of the testator's estate after the payment of all debts, liabilities, other expenses and other legacies. If there is no residuary legacy in the will, this will result in a partial intestacy (see chapter 1).

Generally, the residuary legacy will be worded as a trust for sale. The advantages of doing so are that:

- an express provision avoids the statutory provisions concerning the payment of debts and legacies;
- if the residuary legacy is for persons in succession, an express trust for sale avoids the possible creation of a Settled Land Act settlement; and
- if there are minority interests, an express trust for sale avoids certain problems (see chapter 9).

The only situation where an express trust for sale has no advantages, is if the residue is to go to one person only, and the testator wishes that person to take the property in its present form.

vi) Legacy to a person holding a particular position (eg £100 to my gardener)

If the testator wishes to leave such a legacy, he should be asked:

- whether he wants the legacy to go to that person specifically or whether he wants it to go to the person who holds that position at his death; and
- whether he wants any words of appreciation to be put in the will.

vii) Legacies to institutions (eg £100 to the NSPCC)

If the testator wishes to leave a legacy to an institution, the institution's existence and name should be checked. If it is a charity, its charitable status should be confirmed and the testator should be asked whether he wishes the legacy to be applied cy-pres if the institution is no longer in existence at his death (if so, the 'general charitable intention' of the testator should be expressed in the will).

Provision should be made in the will for the change of name, of objects for the amalgamation or dissolution of the institution.

Provision should also be made for the discharge of the personal representatives. This is done by an express provision that the receipt of a person who appears or professes to be a treasurer or appropriate officer will be sufficient discharge.

f) *Relieving provisions*

i) 'Free of tax'

Although IHT is generally payable out of the residue, if the testator wishes a legacy not to bear tax, an express 'free of tax' provision should be used for clarity.

ii) 'Free of mortgage'

The Administration of Estates Act s35 states that a beneficiary takes property subject to any mortgage over it unless a contrary intention is shown. This is done by the use of an express 'free of mortgage' provision.

iii) 'Free of expenses and costs of transfer'

A beneficiary bears any costs related to a specific gift from the date of the assent, unless contrary intention is shown. This is done by the use of a specific provision.

g) *Dispositions in family cases*

When the testator has a family, it is import to ascertain his priorities as between spouse, children and others, taking into account their own resources.

Considerations include the possibility of each spouse dying first or of a common accident, the spouse's own will and the possible use of a survivorship clause.

Possible dispositions:

i) Absolute gift to spouse with substitutional gifts to the children if the spouse predeceases.

Advantages -

- The spouse is adequately provided for.
- No IHT is payable - the spouse - exemption applies (see chapter 9).
- The spouse is free to make inter vivos transfers, using the applicable exemptions and benefits of potentially exempt transfers (see chapter 9).

Disadvantages -

- Children taking nothing immediately.
- The testator has no control of the ultimate destination of his estate (which means risk if the spouse remarries).
- The testator makes no use of his IHT nil rate band (see chapter 9).
- Spouse may have large estate on death resulting in high IHT liability.

ii) Legacy to children with residue to spouse

Advantages -

- Immediate provision for children.
- Possible use of an Accumulation and Maintenance (A & M) Settlement with IHT benefits (see chapter 9).
- Testator's nil rate band is used.
- Residuary legacy to spouse attracts no IHT - spouse exempt.

Disadvantages -

- If an A & M settlement is created, there will be a charge to CGT when the children become entitled to the capital.
- Possible IHT liability if more than £128,000 is used in legacies for the children.
- The spouse may not be adequately provided for.

iii) Life interest to the spouse, remainder to the children

Advantages -

- Testator retains control over the ultimate destination of his estate.
- There is no charge to IHT on the testator's death; his disposition is spouse-exempt.

Disadvantages -

- Children get nothing immediately.
- The spouse may not be adequately provided for.
- The spouse may have a large estate on death.
- No use of the testator's nil rate band.
- The spouse cannot take advantage of inter vivos exemptions and potentially exempt transfers.

If the chosen disposition is iii), the trustees should be given extra powers - in particular, those of investment of the capital so that a home can be provided for the spouse and children.

h) *Special considerations concerning children*

Distinction between vested and contingent interests:

i) *Vested* - if a child has a vested interest in property, he can claim it on attaining 18 (subject to any life interest). The child has an interest in possession (a present right to present income) throughout.

ii) *Contingent* - the child's interest in the property is contingent upon his attaining a specified age.

(For the tax implications of the distinction, see chapter 9.)

Possibility of further children:

If the testator wishes to benefit children of his who may come into existence after the date of the will, any legacy should be worded as for 'my children' rather than by naming them.

If the testator wishes to benefit others' children who may come into existence after the date of the will, he should express the gift as to a class, and should specify when the class should close (eg 'children of X living at my death').

'Child' includes those 'en ventre sa mère'.

Substitutional gifts:

The testator should consider whether he wishes there to be a substitutional gift in favour of the issue of the children in the event that any of the children predecease the testator.

i) *Executors (and trustees)*

Executors should be expressly appointed.

i) Limitations on appointment

If the executors are also to be trustees or if the estate includes land, at least two executors should be appointed.

A maximum of four executors can take out a grant in respect of each type of property (realty and personalty). If more than four are appointed, the first four will take out the grant and power will be reserved to the other(s) to take the grant if a vacancy arises.

ii) Types of executors:

- Individuals - may be flexible but may lack expertise and may predecease the testator.
- Solicitors or other professionals

  Advantages - expertise; will not predecease.

  Disadvantages - no personal interest; expensive; cautious and inflexible re investments.

  Considerations -

  If a firm is appointed the appointment is construed as an appointment of the partners at the date of the will unless contrary intention is shown. This creates problems if the partners die or retire, so an express provision is necessary, appointing the partners in the firm at the date of death.

  Generally, the provision will specify that only two partners are to take out the grant.

  Express provision should be made for the possibility of an amalgamation or a change of name of the firm.

  A charging clause should be included in the will which should allow the executors to charge for *any* acts which are necessary (including those which a non-professional executor could have done personally).
- Trust corporation or bank

  Advantages - expertise; independence; will not predecease.

  Disadvantages - very expensive; impersonal; cautious and inflexible.

  Considerations - often the corporation will insist that the appointment is made on their standard terms. It should, therefore, be confirmed with the testator that he agrees with these.
- Public trustee

  Advantages - independent; will not predecease; state indemnity.

  Disadvantages - impersonal; very slow; bad investment record; cannot act if believes that the estate is insolvent or if it involves the management of any business.

iii) Considerations when choosing executors:

- Availability, suitability and willingness to act. Generally, executors who are younger than the testator should be appointed.
- If the executor is also a beneficiary, there is a possibility of a conflict of interest unless he is the sole beneficiary.
- It is possible that an executor will predecease the testator so the will should make provision for a substitutional appointment to cover this.
- Expense.
- Other considerations include the size, nature and location of the estate. If it is large or complicated, an expert may need to be appointed.

iv) The appointment of guardians for minors

If the testator has children, this should be considered. An appointment will generally be made conditional on the testator's spouse predeceasing him. If it is not, the guardian and spouse will act jointly.

If a guardian is appointed, the will should provide appropriate financial support. This is usually done by making the guardian trustee of a fund for the children, and extending their powers with regard to the fund including a provision allowing the guardian as trustee to use the fund to purchase a home for the children.

j) *Administrative provisions*

i) Debts and legacies

In general, debts and legacies are automatically paid out of the residue of the estate. However, an express provision to this effect should be included in the will, in order to avoid difficulties which will otherwise result in the event of partial intestacy.

ii) Trustees' powers

Trustees are given various powers by statute. However, these are often limited and it may be advisable to extend them by express provision in the will.

General:

- Power of investment - in general, the statutory powers will be extended to give the trustee power to invest as if he were the sole, absolute, beneficial owner of the property.
- Power to provide capital - Trustee Act 1925 s32 allows trustees to provide capital to a beneficiary who has an interest in the capital but subject to certain limitations. The will may state that these limitations will not apply, and may extend the statutory power to enable the

advancement of capital to beneficiaries who do not have an interest in the capital.

- Powers of insurance - the statutory powers of insurance are provided in Trustee Act 1925 s19, and are very limited. An express provision in the will can remove these limitations.
- Power to purchase a home for beneficiaries - if the testator wishes the trustees to have this power, express provision must be made in the will.
- Power to dispense with the statutory requirement for consents in the event of appropriation - Administration of Estates Act 1925 s41 allows personal representatives to appropriate assets in or towards a legacy, or interest provided that, inter alia, the beneficiary consents. An express provision can be used to dispense with this requirement of consent.

  In addition, if a personal representative is also a beneficiary and wishes to appropriate assets to himself, this would constitute a breach of trust. Express provision can allow such appropriation.
- Power to carry on business - personal representatives only have power to carry on business if they do so in order to sell it as a going concern. If they do so, they can only use assets which were used in the business at the date of death and they are personally liable for all debts incurred (although a right to indemnity from the estate exists). Any or all of these limitations can be removed by express provision in the will.

Where minority interests are involved:

- Trustee Act 1925 s31 and s32 - these provisions allow trustees to advance income and capital for a beneficiary's benefit, subject to limitations. These limitations can be removed by the will (and see chapter 9 post).
- Power to accept receipt of the child's parent or guardian - in general, neither a minor nor his parent or guardian can give a good receipt to trustees for funds advanced to him (with the exception that a married minor *can* give a good receipt). Express provision is, therefore, necessary.

If there is a possibility of the rules on apportionment applying (equitable apportionments and the Apportionment Act 1970) it is generally advisable to specifically exclude them in the will.

k) *Revocation and alteration*

i) Revocation

A will must be revocable until death, although:

- a contract to revoke does not prevent revocation but the testator's estate may be liable for breach of contract.

- the doctrine of mutual wills may render the revocation of a will unconscionable. Mutual wills involve an agreement to make wills in a certain form and not to revoke with the consent of the other. If one party revokes after the death of the other, then on the death of that party, the personal representatives will hold his estate on implied trust for the beneficiary under the agreed mutual wills.

Ways in which a will may be revoked:

- Marriage

  If the testator marries subsequent to the date of the will, the existing will will be revoked unless it appears from the will that (Wills Act 1837 s18):

  At the time the will was made, the testator was expecting to be married to the particular person; *and*

  He intended that the will (or that a disposition in the will) should not be revoked by the contemplated marriage.

  Therefore, if the testator is contemplating marriage and wishes to avoid the above effects, an express clause should be included at the beginning of the will.

- Divorce

  If the testator is divorced subsequent to the date of the will:

  The will takes effect as if any appointment of the former spouse as executor or trustee is omitted; *and*

  Any gift to the former spouse lapses. This means that the former spouse is not treated as if he has predeceased the testator, and so any substitutional gift to take effect on the former spouse predeceasing is ineffective and the property will pass to the residuary beneficiaries or, if none, according to the rules of intestacy.

  The exception to this is where the gift to the former spouse is of a life interest. In this case, in the event of divorce, the interests of the remaindermen are simply accelerated and their interests fall into possession immediately as if the former spouse had predeceased the testator.

- Destruction of the will

  Wills Act 1837 s20 provides that if the will is burnt or torn or otherwise destroyed by the testator or by some person in his presence and by his direction and with the intention of revoking it, then the will is thereby revoked.

  Mental capacity - the testator must have mental capacity at the time of destruction. If the will is found mutilated, intention is presumed.

Symbolic destruction - is not sufficient; nor is it sufficient simply to write on the will that it has been revoked. The testator must have done all that he intended to do by way of revocation.

The destruction must be of a sufficiently vital part in order to infer intention to defer the whole. If it is not, there will be partial revocation of the part destroyed.

The destruction of a will does not destroy subsequent codicils.

The will last known to be in the testator's possession and which can not be found at his death is presumed to be revoked subject to contrary evidence.

The dependent relative doctrine - if the court is satisfied that the testator intended the revocation to be conditional, the revocation will not be effective if the condition is not satisfied.

- By a later will or codicil

  Any will should include an express clause revoking all previous wills and testamentary dispositions. If there is none, the previous will or codicil will be impliedly revoked by the later will in so far as the later will contradicts or repeats the former.

ii) Alteration

Alteration of a will after its execution is invalid unless:

- the alteration is executed in the same way as the will (the initials of the testator and the witnesses will be sufficient); or
- the will is subsequently re-executed or is confirmed by a codicil which refers to the alteration.

The presumption is that alterations (but *not* completed blanks) were made after the execution. This presumption can be rebutted by evidence such as the initialling of the alterations.

If the alteration is not valid, the effect is:

- if the original wording is 'apparent' (ie can be deciphered by natural means) then that wording will be admitted to probate.
- if the original wording is not apparent, then:

  if the original wording can be ascertained by extrinsic evidence, it will be admitted to probate; or

  if it can not be ascertained, probate will be granted with a blank space.

3 FAMILY PROVISION

3.1 Introduction

The Inheritance (Provision for Family and Dependants) Act 1975 (IPFDA) allows the court to vary the terms of a will or the provisions on intestacy. Thus, anyone who feels 'hard done by' can apply to the court for provision under the IPFDA provided that the Act gives them locus standi to do so.

3.2 Key points

By s1(1), if the deceased died domiciled in England and Wales, a person can apply to the court for a s2 order on the ground that the disposition of the deceased's estate by will, or the law relating to intestacy, or both: 'is not such as to make reasonable financial provision for the applicant'.

a) *Who can apply?*

i) Spouse of the deceased (including judicially separated spouse and a party to a void marriage).

ii) Former spouse of the deceased who has not remarried (NB: though that where the parties have settled their financial affairs on divorce, there must be exceptional circumstances to show that reasonable provision has not been made for the spouse).

(NB: re (i) and (ii) above, IPFDA s15 provides that the court, on a decree of divorce or nullity or judicial separation can, if it thinks it just and both parties agree, order that either party is barred from making an application under the Act.)

iii) Child (including an illegitimate or legitimated or adopted child or one en ventre sa mére) of the deceased. (NB: though, that the court is not very sympathetic to applications from adult able employed children.)

iv) Any person who was treated by the deceased as a child of the family concerning any marriage to which the deceased was a party.)

v) Any person who, immediately before the death of the deceased, was maintained wholly or partially by him.

Section 1(3) - a person was maintained by the deceased if the latter made a substantial contribution in money or money's worth towards his reasonable needs other than for full valuable consideration. This is a question of fact.

b) '*Reasonable financial provision*' means is it reasonable, taking into account the applicant's position and needs at the date of the hearing?

i) Standards

- for a spouse (unless judicially separated) the court must look to what provision is itself reasonable. The spouse's needs are irrelevant and the spouse should receive at least what they would receive on divorce.
- for others, the court must see what would constitute reasonable provision for their maintenance.

ii) Guidelines (for the court):

- Financial resources and needs of the applicant and of the other beneficiaries.
- Deceased's moral obligations to the applicant.
- Size and nature of the estate.
- Physical or mental disability of the applicant and of the other beneficiaries.
- Any other relevant information eg any lifetime provision by the deceased, conduct of the applicant, if relevant, the source of the deceased's property.
- Spouse applicant - age, duration of marriage, contribution to welfare or family, provision could expect on divorce.
- Child applicant - manner in which they might expect to be educated or trained.
- Child of the family applicant - as for the child applicant (above) plus the extent to which the deceased assumed responsibility for their maintenance.

c) *Orders*

Orders are made against the 'Net Estate' - s2:

i) Property the deceased could have disposed of by will less funeral, testamentary and administrative expenses, debts and liabilities.

ii) Property the deceased could have appointed inter vivos by a general power which was not exercised.

iii) Nominations - a direction to a body who hold funds for the deceased to pay the funds to a nominated person on the deceased's death. The limit is £5,000, the nomination must be in writing and the nominator must be over 16. (Nominations are revoked by subsequent marriage, by a later nomination, and by the death of the nominee.)

iv) Donationes Mortis Causa (DMC) - a gift made in contemplation of death and conditional on death. It is only possible with personalty and the deceased must have handed over the property or a means of attaining it to the donee. (DMCs are revoked if the donor recovers from the contemplated cause of death and if he resumes possession and dominion over the property.)

Plus, if the court so orders:

v) Deceased's share of a joint tenancy.

vi) Property covered by anti-avoidance legislation - inter vivos gifts within six years of death and contracts to leave property by will at anytime before death if the intention was to defeat a claim under the Act and full valuable consideration was not given.

d) *Types of order*

i) Periodical payments for any period

ii) Lump sum

iii) Transfer of property

iv) Settlement of property

v) Order PRs to purchase property and to transfer it to the applicant

vi) Variation of marriage settlement

e) *Effect of order*

Burden can be thrown on any part of the estate. The order is deemed effective from death, and the property is treated as if it had devolved on the deceased's death subject to the provisions of the order.

f) *Other*

A summon must be issued six months from the grant. The court can give leave to issue after this period if there is a special reason for the delay - but the PRs will be protected if they wait six months before distributing the estate.

A statement by the deceased as to why he did not make reasonable financial provision is admissible in evidence. Such a statement should be put with the will but not in it.

4 QUESTIONS (PRE-DEATH)

QUESTION 1

Please read and consider carefully the will of John Jones which is set out below. John Jones has a substantial estate. He and his wife are in their mid-forties and have three children aged 15, 12 and nine.

If, in answering the following questions (except part (f)), you consider that the existing relevant provisions of the will should be amended or new ones made, set out what you would suggest. You need not follow the precise words of any precedents as long as the substance and effect of what you propose is clear and appropriate.

(a) (i) Explain the statutory background to and purpose of the survivorship period in clause 1. Please also deal with any relevant considerations.

11 marks

(ii) Explain whether clause 1 as drawn presents any potential problems regarding the operation of the remaining provisions of the will.

4 marks

(b) Explain and comment on the nature and effect of the legacies in sub-clauses 4.1, 4.2 and 4.3 and draw attention to any problems posed by them.

10 marks

4 marks (c) What will be the effect of the gift in clause 4.4 and why?

(d) Explain any difficulty which you foresee regarding the gift in clause 4.5, and how it might be overcome. You should assume that the Association exists at death and is not a charity.

6 marks

(e) State in what respect the introductory words of clause 5 (ie up to the colon) depart from normal practice.

4 marks

(f) Comment generally on the gifts in clauses 5(a) and 5(b). Your answer should include a reference to the distinction between vested and contingent gifts.

In the case of this part question only there is no need in your present answer to set out any suggestions you might have for amendment of or addition to the present wording.

7 marks

3 marks (g) Explain the relevance or otherwise of clause 6.

(h) What are the formal requirements for the attestation of a will? In this context, comment on the clause in this will. What will be the effect of execution as shown here?

9 marks

---

58 marks

Law Society Solicitors' Final Examination
Wills, Probate and Administration Summer 1986 Q1

This Will dated 2nd January 1983 is made by me, John Jones of 4 Church Street, Sutton, Nottinghamshire and revokes all former wills.

1 If my wife, Hilda Jones, survives me by 30 days, I give the whole of my estate to her and appoint her to be my sole executrix but if she does not so survive me then the following provisions of this Will shall apply.

2.1 I appoint as my executors and trustees my brother Fred Jones of 1 North Street, Sutton and my solicitor Michael Mann of Bank Chambers, Sutton.

2.2 In this Will the expression 'my trustees' means my executors and the trustees of this Will and any trusts arising under it.

3 I appoint my brother Fred Jones and my sister Elizabeth Jones as guardians of any of my children who are under 18.

4 I give the following legacies:

4.1 £1,000 to my solicitor, Michael Mann. general legacy

4.2 The cash which is in the safe in my study at my death to my friend, William Warner of 4 Potter Street, Watford. – specific legacy

4.3 £500 to my sister Elizabeth Jones to be paid out of my deposit account with the Sutton Building Society. – demonstrative legacy

4.4 If my death occurs while I am travelling by air and I have at the time a policy of insurance which is payable on death during such travel, the proceeds of that policy to the beneficiaries named in a note which I shall give to my solicitor and in the shares there stated.

4.5 £1,000 to the Sutton Old Comrades' Association.

5 My trustees shall divide the rest of my estate and pay it as follows:

(a) Nine-tenths to my children.

(b) One-tenth to my sister Susan Jones.

6 All income received after my death shall be treated as income of my estate regardless of the period to which it relates and the statutory rules concerning apportionment and the rules in *Howe* v *Dartmouth* and *Allhusen* v *Whittell* shall not be applied.

[7 etc...............

Note to candidates - the Will here continues with appropriate powers of executors (including to charge) which are not relevant to the questions asked.]

Signed by the testator	)	Signature of John Jones
Signed by Hilda Andrews	)	
Secretary with Michael Mann & Co,	)	Signature of Hilda Andrews
Solicitors, Sutton	)	
Signed by Joyce Paling,		
Secretary with Michael Mann & Co,	)	Signature of Joyce Paling
Solicitors, Sutton		

QUESTION 1 - SOLUTION

General comment

This was an unimaginative question of considerable simplicity where it was not surrounded by ambiguity. Both sub-questions 1(e) and 1(f) presented the now familiar problem to the student of identifying precisely what it was that the examiner was looking for. Question 1(b), for nine marks, asking for the formal requirements for the attestation of a will, appeared unbelievably simple - and was.

Suggested solution

a) i) The statutory background to, and purpose of, the survivorship period in clause 1 of the Will should be seen in the context of its consequences as regards both succession and inheritance tax.

After having considered the possibility of Mrs Jones dying shortly after him, Mr Jones has presumably agreed to the insertion of the survivorship clause for the purpose of retaining control over the destination of his estate and with a view to avoiding the delay and expense of double administration.

The usual 30-day period anticipates not only actual survival by a short period, but also the notional survival which is deemed to occur in the circumstances of s184 Law of Property Act 1925 - that is, that if two or more persons die in circumstances such that there is no evidence as to which was the survivor, then for the purposes of succession to property the younger is deemed to have survived the elder. Accordingly, a gift by the elder to the younger would devolve as part of the latter's estate.

It is not known whether Mrs Jones is in fact younger than her husband: if she is, the survival of Mrs Jones will not entitle her personal representatives to claim under the will if she dies within 30 days of her husband.

A more vexed situation could arise if her death occurred within that period and there was a partial or total failure of the residuary bequest made under the will. If Mrs Jones survived by only a few days the undisposed of property would pass to her estate under the intestacy rules. If the order of deaths was uncertain then her estate would have no claim under the intestacy rules, because of s46(3) Administration of Estates Act 1925. This provision states that s184 (supra) does not apply as between husband and wife if the elder dies wholly or partly intestate, the result being here that the property passing under the intestacy of the elder (Mr Jones) would devolve as though the younger (Mrs Jones) had not survived.

As regards IHT consequences, if the clause is retained and Mrs Jones survives the required period the transfer to her of her husband's entire estate would be exempt because of the spouse: however, if exemption she survives him only to die within 30 days IHT will be chargeable as if she had acquired no interest in his property. IHT will thus be payable on the death of the first spouse to die but none will be payable on the death of the second spouse.

If the clause is deleted then no IHT will be payable on the death of the first spouse to die because of the spouse exemption but there will be IHT to pay on the death of the second.

Whether or not the survivorship clause is retained, if the order of deaths is uncertain both are deemed to die at the same instant: IHT would only be payable on the death of the elder.

ii) As drawn, clause 1 will present problems regarding the operation of the remaining provisions of the will should John Jones's marriage end in annulment or dissolution. Section 18(2) Administration of Justice Act 1982 inserted a new s18A to the Wills Act 1837 to the effect that if a marriage is dissolved or annulled the will is to take effect as if any appointment of the former spouse as executor, or as executor and trustee, were omitted. Further, any devise or bequest to the former spouse lapses and, in the absence of a substitutional gift, the property given to the former spouse will fall into residue or if itself a gift of residue pass under intestacy. In *Re Sinclair* (1985) the Court of Appeal decided that where a will containing a gift to the spouse of a testator fails because of their divorce a gift over in the event of the spouse's death will be ineffective. The same applies to the appointment.

One way to overcome this difficulty would be to alter the wording, as follows: 'But if this gift fails for any reason then the following provisions of this will shall apply instead of this clause'. The 'following provisions' will then apply whether the failure results from death or any other reason.

b) The legacies in clauses 4.1, 4.2 and 4.3 are respectively general, specific and demonstrative. It is not expressly stated whether they are tax free. It is common to state this, even though in its absence the tax will be paid in accordance with the order for application of assets under the Administration of Estates Act 1925, Part II

Schedule I, which in practice will mean from the residuary estate or, in priority, undisposed of residue, if any.

Clause 4.1 creates a general legacy, pecuniary in form; it consists of property in no way distinguished from other property of the same kind; the beneficiary will be entitled regardless of whether there is actual cash available to meet the payment; if there is none it will have to be raised by the executors out of residue. The legacy does not make it clear whether it is conditional upon the solicitor proving the will. Although this is implied it is better to cover the provision expressly whatever the intention may be. Beyond this there remains the question of professional ethics. The Council of the Law Society have decided - and see *Re a Solicitor* (1975) - that a solicitor must refuse to act where a testator proposes to make a gift of a significant amount (either in itself or having regard to the size of the testator's estate or to other normal claims on his bounty) to the solicitor, or to a partner, staff or their families. It is, however, permissible for the solicitor to act in drafting a will by which he receives a token legacy as a mark of the testator's appreciation. A sum of £1,000 is not initially likely to be regarded as a token legacy but much will depend on the size of the estate. Here the estate is described as 'substantial'. It could be that the legacy is, indeed, a token. It would have been preferable for words such as 'as a mark of my appreciation' to have been used. This would have helped towards raising the desired presumption. A further point is that the will would lack 'knowledge and approval' until such time as any suspicions circumstances were removed - see *Wintle* v *Nye* (1959).

The gift in clause 4.2 is a specific legacy, being clearly distinguished from other property of the same kind. If there is no money in the safe at death William Warner will take nothing because the doctrine of ademption will apply.

The gift in clause 4.3, being expressed to be payable from a particular fund, is demonstrative. The effect is that it remains payable even if the fund no longer exists at the testator's death. It may be that specific provision should have been included to cover this possibility but this is not essential.

c) An unsuccessful attempt has been made to incorporate a document by reference, namely the note. It will have no effect as a codicil unless it is itself duly executed like a will. For an unexecuted document to be incorporated by reference it must be in existence at the date of the execution of the will; it must be referred to in the will as being in existence; and it must be possible clearly to identify the document concerned. Here the testator has used the word 'shall', thereby implying the existence of a document that may not get be in existence and which is certainly not identified as already being in existence. Any policy monies will form part of the residuary estate.

d) A number of possible difficulties emerge with this particular gift in clause 4.5, as follows:

   i) Because of problems of identification an address should have been included.

ii) Provision ought to have been made for any change of name or objects, amalgamation or dissolution.

iii) The association is unincorporated and so a provision should have been included in the will for the discharge of the trustees on making payment.

In order to cover the deficiencies of (ii) and (iii) the following provision should have been included: 'If the Association changes its name or amalgamates with or transfers its assets to any other body then my trustees shall give effect to this body as if it had been made to the body in its changed name or which results from the amalgamation or to which the transfer has been made. The receipt of a person who appears to be a proper officer of the Association shall be a discharge to my trustees'.

e) There is a departure from usual practice in so far as residue is not expressed to be held on trust for sale and there is no direction for payment out of the proceeds of debts, capital transfer tax, executorship and legacies.

f) With regard to clause 5(a), there is no express closing of the class. This necessitates application of the somewhat artificial class-closing rules, the effect of which will be to close the class at the testator's death. All those children of the testator living or en ventre sa mere will constitute the class.

Further, no method of division is stated, in which case an equal division will be implied. With regard to the possibility of lapse arising s33 Wills Act 1837, as substituted by s19 Administration of Justice Act 1982, will save the gift from lapsing into residue if any of the children die before the testator leaving issue living at the date of the testator's death; the gift will then take effect as one to issue then living. Once there has been survival the gift will have vested and its destination on the child's death will depend upon the child's will or intestacy (necessarily the latter if death occurs earlier than 18). Where the interest is vested it will be in the child's estate for the purpose of any IHT on his death.

There is no specific difficulty as regards clause 5(b), as such, but without a provision for accruer or substitution the gift will lapse if Susan Jones dies before the executor. The will ought to contain an express substitutional clause and not rely on the saving effect of s33. There should also be a final gift over by way of longstop provision.

The chief distinction between vested and contingent gifts is that the latter create no entitlement until the condition attached to the gift is satisfied. Contingent gifts may create a perpetuity. Vested gifts, of their nature, cannot do so. Vested gifts may be vested in possession (immediate entitlement) or vested in interest (postponed entitlement, such as a vested remainder).

g) Clause 6 is irrelevant here. It would only be relevant to exclude the operation of the apportionment rules where, but for exclusion, an apportionment would have to be made by the personal representatives of the deceased's estate - that is, where residuary personalty is left to persons in succession. Here no life-interest is created and so the clause is therefore not required.

h) The attestation clause does not meet the requirements of the Wills Act 1837. By s9 Wills Act, the will must be in writing and signed by the testator or someone in his presence and by his direction; the testator's signature must be made or acknowledged in the presence of at least two witnesses present at the same time; the signature must show that the testator intended to give effect to the will by signing it; each witness must either attest and sign the will or acknowledge his signature in the presence of the testator but not necessarily in the presence of any other witness.

The attestation clause here does not show that these requirements have been satisfied. A short-form attestation clause would be appropriate: 'Signed by the testator in our joint presence and then by us in his'.

An attestation clause is not required to validate the will but to obviate the need for production to the registrar of affidavit of due execution from one or both of the witnesses showing that the will has, in fact, been duly executed.

QUESTION 2

As a partner in A, B & C, solicitors of Northtown, you are consulted by X who lives with his girlfriend Y. They have no plans to marry.

X and Y have one child, a daughter.

X was previously married (the marriage was dissolved some years ago) to W, by whom he has two other children.

All the children are minors. There are no other relatives.

(a) Answer, with explanations, the following questions which X asks you:

(i) 'Who will be entitled to my estate if I die without making a will?

10 marks

(ii) If I make a will leaving half my estate equally between my ex-wife and my two children by her and half equally between Y and our daughter, could the will be challenged? If it could be challenged on what grounds might this successfully be done and by whom and are there any precautions you would advise me to take regarding this?'

18 marks

(b) What are:

(i) the potential capital gains tax consequences and

(ii) the potential capital transfer tax consequences

of X not marrying Y and how serious are these?

8 marks

(c) On the assumption that X decides to make a will:

(i) How would you advise him regarding the appointment of executors and trustees? Please in your answer deal in general terms with the number of executors, the possibility of their being trustees as well, the difference possible appointees, their relative merits and the factors that influence the choice.

(ii) Would it be possible to appoint as executors and trustees A, B & C as a firm and if so, how?

(iii) If you, as a partner in A, B & C, were asked to act as an executorwhat, if any, special provision would you include in the will and what, if any, precautions would you take regarding execution?

8 marks

(d) Prepare for the guidance of your staff a note of the information required when they take instructions for a will, of the typical possible dispositions in family cases and the special considerations in respect of gifts to children.

11 marks

67 marks

Law Society Solicitors' Final Examination
Wills, Probate and Administration Winter 1987 Q1

QUESTION 2 - SOLUTION

General comment

This question should have presented no problem at all to the averagely-prepared student. It is further confirmation that the examiner is finding it difficult to invent new themes to questions. For 67 marks, sub-divided into four parts, parts (b) and (c) have appeared in previous papers, part (c) in three earlier papers (while part (d), for 11 marks, involved nothing more than regurgitating three pages of core material. Part (a)(i) for ten marks was unbelievably simple: it seems difficult to envisage how any student can have failed to secure a very high mark even with only a rudimentary knowledge of the law of intestacy: part (a)(ii) invited candidates to consider the feasibility of a family provision application, but on facts so sparse that it is difficult to know what the examiner can have been expecting in the 18 marks allotted, other than fairly basic material.

Suggested solution

a) i) If X dies without making a will the laws of intestacy will apply to his estate. Section 33 Administration of Estates Act 1925 provides that the estate will be administered by his personal representatives on the footing that all property will vest in them on statutory trust for sale, to be distributed in accordance with the provisions of s46 AEA. As there is no surviving spouse and there are no relatives other than two children of his former marriage to W, and the one child of his illicit union with Y (which is therefore illegitimate), the pv's (who may prove difficult to ascertain on the facts given) will hold all X's estate on the statutory trusts of the AEA for the three children; this means contingently until any such child attains 18, or marries hereunder. If any such child fails to attain a vested interest, as described, his or her share will accrue to such child that does. No distinction, for this purpose, is made between the two legitimate children of the former marriage and the illegitimate child.

ii) The will could be challenged by a family provision application made under the Inheritance (Provision for Family and Dependents) Act 1975. The possible claimants are the former wife, W, provided that she has not remarried: s1(1)(b), and the children of X: s1(1)(c). It may also be possible for Y to bring a claim under s1(1)(e).

An application can be made for an order under s2 on the ground that the disposition of the deceased's estate effected by his will is not such as to make reasonable financial provision for the applicant.

So far as W is concerned for herself, the basis of her claim would be reasonable provision for her maintenance, and the court would pay regard to the common guidelines imposed by the statute - financial resources and needs of W, of other applicants and of the beneficiaries of X's estate; the deceased's moral obligations to W; the size and nature of the estate; any physical or mental disability of W, or any other beneficiary; and anything else relevant, such as conduct of the applicant or lifetime provision made by the deceased.

W would seek to argue that one-half shared between three persons, ie one-sixth in all, is not reasonable provision for her maintenance. The facts given do not lead to a conclusion one way or the other: in W's case the court might be concerned to examine the source from which X derived his assets: if W was able to establish that she made a substantial contribution to the size of X's estate she might have a better claim: see *Sivyer* v *Sivyer* (1967). W's claim necessarily fails, however, if she has remarried at the time of the application.

So far as the two children of X are concerned their claim would be brought by their 'next friend', their mother. The same common guidelines would apply but additionally the court would pay regard to the manner in which the applicants were being, or in which they might expect to be, educated or trained.

Y's claim would rest on s1(1)(c), as being a person who immediately before the death of X was being maintained, either wholly or partly, by the deceased. Section 1(3) provides that a person is 'maintained' by the deceased if the deceased made a substantial contribution in money or money's worth towards his reasonable needs, otherwise than for valuable consideration.

Under the terms of X's will Y would obtain one-third of the net estate: whether she would successfully claim more would depend upon the court's examination of the criteria in the common guidelines, together with the special guideline appropriate to s1(1)(c) claims - the extent to which, and the basis upon which, the deceased assumed responsibility for the applicant's maintenance and the length of time for which the deceased discharged that responsibility.

Application must be made not later than six months from the grant of representation to the estate, or later with leave of the court.

The precaution that should be given to X when he comes to prepare his will, or when he comes to instruct another to prepare the will for him, is that a written statement should be placed alongside his will explaining why he may not have made 'reasonable financial provision' for a possible applicant. This would then be admissible in evidence.

b) i) *X and Y remaining unmarried: the capital gains tax position*

Capital gains tax is charged upon the gains made from a chargeable disposal. The gains are calculated by deducting from the consideration for which the assets are disposed the following: the acquisition costs; subsequent expenditure incurred in enhancing the value of the assets; and incidental costs incurred in disposal of the assets. If the assets are given away, inter vivos, then the consideration received for them will be deemed to be their market value at the time of disposal. Such gifts made to each other by X and Y will be subject to CGT at their normal income tax rates.

On death, however, no CGT is payable. If X or Y left a gift to the other by will the donee will be deemed to acquire the asset at its market value at death, without incurring a charge to CGT. If the donee was deemed to require the goods at the donor's acquisition costs this could result in the donee being required to pay more CGT on subsequent disposal of the asset as it would then have a lower base value and so the gain made on the disposal would be greater than if the receipt was one based on market value. An annual exemption of £5,000 is available in respect of chargeable gains.

ii) *X and Y remaining unmarried: the inheritance tax position*

Inheritance tax on lifetime gifts is charged upon chargeable transfers of value. Tax will be charged upon the value transferred by such transfers and this value will be the amount by which the estate is diminished as a result of the transfer. Gifts are potentially chargeable transfers and so will only attract a charge to IHT if the transferor dies within seven years. IHT is a cumulative tax and the rate of tax will depend upon the amount of chargeable transfers made by the transferor in the previous seven years. There is an annual exemption of £3,000 and unused exemption can be carried forward for one year. Upon death the deceased is deemed to make a chargeable transfer of his whole estate. Any chargeable transfers (including potentially chargeable) made by the deceased within seven years of the deceased's death will also attract IHT. Thus, if X or Y left property to the other by will upon death it would be subject to IHT. The IHT nil rate band of £128,000 would still be available provided lifetime transfers within the previous seven years have not exhausted it, but there are no annual exemptions.

c) i) When advising a client on the question of whom to appoint, the first point to consider is convenience, and the client's own wishes. If the will is a simple one it will usually be best to advise the client to appoint the spouse or, as here, the cohabitee as executrix. However, you should advise the client that if the named person should fail to survive he should consider an alternative appointment, and you should make such provision in the will to cater for such an event.

In other cases you should advise the client that there is a choice between individuals (who will usually be persons desired by the client), solicitors or other professional persons, Trust Corporations and Banks and the Public Trustee.

Individuals should only be chosen if they are trustworthy, suitable, willing and resident in this country. Unless the will is one where the executor is also the sole beneficiary, it is preferable not to appoint an executor who is also a beneficiary to avoid any potential conflict of interest. Individuals may, of course, predecease the testator, so that substitutional appointments may be needed. If no such provision is made, and the executor does predecease the testator, the arbitrary provisions of NCPR need to be relied upon. If the estate is a small and simple one it is best to appoint ordinary individuals to avoid excessive costs and charges depleting the value of the estate.

In the case of the appointment of solicitors or professional persons, it will be necessary to provide in the will for a charging clause. As in the case of individuals, these persons (or their firm if appointed), must consent and must be available and suitable for the task. The advantage of appointing a Trust Corporation or a Bank is that there will be complete impartiality in administration, and the expertise of the Corporation's Department, which should be skilled in executor and trust business, will be available. Such an appointment will be on the institution's standard terms and conditions. The disadvantage of such an appointment lies in the area of cost, which may turn out to be particularly onerous in the case of a small estate, and in the nature of the institutions themselves where because of their size, matters tend to be delegated and may take some considerable time to be dealt with. The Public Trustee is usually considered very much as a last resort; his scale of charges is higher than most bank trust departments, and he may not consent to be appointed in certain cases. The advantage of the Public Trustee is that as a Government Department there is complete impartiality and it is skilled in probate administration work, although this is balanced to a certain extent by the possibility of delays and delegation which may be encountered in the Public Trustee Office.

It is usually advisable to appoint two executors if they are to be trustees; they will be trustees in all cases where the will does not provide for immediate vesting in absolutely entitled beneficiaries. Where there is land comprised in a trust it will be essential to have not less than two trustees (or a trust corporation), to receive the purchase money on a sale in order to overreach the beneficial interests. Not more than four executors can take a grant; power will be reserved for the others to take when necessary. Where the client is an author, playright, or musician it will be necessary to consider the appointment of a person to act as executor of his literary (or other) works. Where trusts are created by the will it is invariable and convenient to make the same persons executors and trustees. Where there is settled land and where the settlement is not to come to an end on the death of the client, it is necessary to consider the need to appoint special personal representatives.

ii) It is possible to appoint a firm of solicitors as executors. If so, it is necessary to make it plain in the appointment clause that the appointment is of *the partners at the date of death.* If this were not done, it would take effect as an appointment of the partners at the date of the will. It is also desirable to prevent difficulties from arising by virtue of a reconstruction or amalgamation of the firm by providing that the appointment will cover any firm which may at the date of the death be carrying on the practice of the firm names. Anything more radical in the nature of a change (such as a complete dissolution), will not be capable of cover, and if this is likely to arise, you should advise the testator accordingly so that he may reconsider his position. Where the firm is appointed the partners will decide which of them will prove the will, and this cannot be dictated by the testator. If he wishes to dictate which partners shall prove he can only do so by appointing them in his will by name.

There will, in such an appointment, be the usual professional charging clause. And, see further, *Re Horgan* (1971).

iii) I would include the usual professional charging clause. I would ensure that the witnesses were not either:

- the person or persons named as executors; or
- likely to become executors named in any future codicil.

Accordingly, they should be typists, clerks or secretaries, or other persons not likely ever to become executors under the clause. If this were not so the rule contained in s15 Wills Act 1837 (as amended by s1 Wills Act 1968), which prevents an attesting witness taking a benefit under the will, would apply. Such a benefit would include a power to charge under a clause in the will; hence the need to avoid the person being entitled to charge being an attesting witness.

d) i) The information required for staff when they take instructions for a will would embrace the following matters:

- *Is there an existing will?* If so, check whether or not it has been revoked. If only small changes are contemplated consider use of a codicil, rather than a new will.
- *Who comprise the testator's family and dependants*, and what are their needs and resources? Bear in mind the possibility of any claim being brought under Inheritance (Provision for Family and Dependants) Act 1975.

- *Nature and composition of the estate*

  What is the size of the estate?

  What types of property will be eligible for taxation relief?

  What types of property do not pass by will?

  Joint property; nominated property; insurance policies for the benefit of other persons, eg under Married Women's Property Act 1882 s11; pension benefits.

- *Have there been any lifetime transfers*? Calculate the testator's cumulative total of transfers, and consider financial planning in general when taking instructions for the will. Can the testator afford to dispose of some of his estate by lifetime transfer, making use of lifetime exemptions?

- *Review*. A reminder that wills should be kept under review, particularly where there have been changes in the tax laws or in the testator's personal circumstances, such as divorce.

ii) Possible dispositions in family cases include:

- *Generally ascertaining the testator's priorities* as between spouse, children and others, taking into account their own resources, and contemplating the possibility of each spouse dying first, and of common accident. The spouse's own estate and will should be taken into account: use of a survivorship clause may mitigate the problem.

- *Absolute gift to spouse* with a substitutional gift to children should spouse predecease.

  With this arrangement the testator may lose the benefit of his own nil rate band if spouse survives, but control over ultimate destination of property is transferred to spouse, if he or she survives.

- *Legacy to children, residue to spouse*. Subject to making adequate provision for spouse and subject to previous chargeable transfers the testator may give to children a legacy equivalent to the size of the nil rate band in force from time to time without incurring capital transfer tax liability.

- *Life interest to spouse, remainder to children*. This may not provide adequately for the spouse's needs. Consider the inclusion of powers for trustees to make advances of capital and/or loans to spouse. However, the testator retains control over disposition of estate on spouse's death. Consider, further, other additional administrative powers, particularly the extention of trustees' powers of investment to cover provision of a home for spouse and children.

iii) Special considerations in respect of gifts to children.

If the gift to a child is absolute it vests on testator's death and the child may claim the property (subject to any life-interest given to spouse) on attaining 18. Until then the child is not able to give a valid receipt, so if the testator wishes to postpone the child's enjoyment of the gift until he attains an age greater than 18, the gift should be made contingent upon the child's attaining the required age.

Consideration should be given to the possibility of further children. Provision may be made by a gift by description instead of by name. The date when the class closes should be specified, thereby overriding the class closing rules.

Consideration, further, should be given to a substitutional gift to grandchildren or issue should a child predecease. The usual provision is for distribution 'per stirpes', the children of a deceased child dividing his share between them - rather than 'per capita' - the children of the deceased child sharing equally with the surviving children.

QUESTION 3

For the purpose of this question the provisions of the Family Provision (Intestate Succession) Order 1987 (SI 1987/779) (ie increases in statutory legacies on intestacy with effect from 1 June 1987) should be ignored.

You are consulted by Bill Jones about the possibility of his making a will. He has come to see you somewhat reluctantly because, as he puts it, 'my understanding is that if I do nothing everything will surely go to my wife and then to the boys, which is what I want'.

Mr Jones is married to Hilda and they have two children, Michael (aged 17) and Peter (eight).

Mr Jones tells you that his estate comprises:

Asset	Approximate value £
Matrimonial home at	
1 Kings Road, St Sampsons	90,000
Personal chattels	5,000
Investments and cash	75,000

He also says that on his death while in the service of his present employers (XYZ Limited) there will be a lump sum, payable at the discretion of the trustees of the firm's pension fund, which at present would amount to £100,000. He has no insurance policies.

You ask if he has any liabilities. He replies that an outstanding mortgage is secured on the matrimonial home. A sum of £20,000 is still owing.

You also ask about Mrs Jones. Mr Jones says that whatever might be said about his making a will there is certainly no need for her to make one; it would just, in his view, be a waste of money. Apart from a few personal belongings she has absolutely nothing: not even a bank account.

(a) (i) Particularly in view of his wishes as expressed above explain why Mr Jones should indeed, make a will.

(ii) As at Mr Jones's death what is the inheritance tax position under his will if he leaves his wife:

(A) a life interest?

(B) an absolute interest?

(iii) Ignoring inheritance tax considerations, compare and contrast the advantages and disadvantages (so far as both Mrs Jones and the children are concerned) of Mr Jones leaving his wife a life interest and an absolute interest under his will.

(iv) Explain the relevance to Mr Jones' lifetime inheritance tax planning of the the discretionary payment under the pension fund of XYZ Limited.

14 marks

(b) Explain briefly whether you would advise that any action should be taken regarding Mrs Jones: whether anything could be done about her position during Mr Jones' life and whether she should make a will.

7 marks

(c) On the assumption that Mr Jones decides to instruct you to prepare a will for him leaving everything to his wife absolutely if she survives him by 30 days but otherwise to his sons equally at 18, appointing you, his solicitor (to be described as ABC), and his brother (George Jones) as executors:

(i) Are there any standard provisions dealing with the powers of the executors which in your opinion should be included in the will? There is no need to draft the relevant clauses; you should merely state briefly what they are and their purpose.

(ii) Why should the gift to Mrs Jones should be conditional on her surviving by 30 days? What other matter would you have in mind in relation to the possible failure of the gift to Mrs Jones?

(iii) What considerations of a succession nature would you discuss with Mr Jones regarding his proposed gift to the sons?

18 marks

(d) Ignoring any administrative provisions suggested in your answer to (c)(i), set out in your own words a draft of the will you would suggest for Mr Jones. You should bear in mind, so far as the gift to Mrs Jones and the children are concerned, the considerations you have mentioned in your answer to (c)(ii) and (iii). Precise drafting in accordance with precedents is not necessary as long as what you produce is clear and effective.

15 marks

---

54 marks

Law Society Solicitors' Final Examination
Wills, Probate and Administration Summer 1987 Q1

QUESTION 3 - SOLUTION

General comment

This was a pre-death question of a type which students have encountered in previous examinations. The policy now seems finally settled to have one such question in the paper and one post-death question. The difficulty for the examiner is inventing new themes and avoiding predictability. On the whole the question was well-balanced but there is always some doubt in the candidate's mind about a requirement to 'explain briefly'. How brief should brief be? For seven marks (Question 3(b)) an answer should strike the right balance. The will draft, for 15 marks, ought to have presented no serious problems: never the less the point remains that candidates ought not in a practical examination, to be given the option to write a will in their own words.

Suggested solution

a) i) It is not completely clear as to Mr Jones's wishes. He wants to benefit his wife and children but does not indicate what their respective shares might be. The use of the word 'then' is ambiguous: it could mean that he wishes his wife to take a life-interest but on the other hand it may not have this interpretation at all: indeed, if he expressed himself in this way in a home-made will s22 Administration of Justice Act 1982 would operate to make the gift to his wife absolute. Perhaps, in fact, he would only wish his children to take if his wife does not survive him.

It is advisable for Mr Jones to make a will for the following reasons:

- If he does not do so and his children survive him his widow will only receive the personal chattels, as defined under s55(1)(x) AEA, a statutory legacy of £75,000 and a life-interest in half the residue. Any rights she might have to appropriate the matrimonial home in satisfaction of her legacy, or capitalise the life-interest, will not have a very beneficial effect on the facts of this estate. The children's entitlement will be on the statutory trusts as to half the residue and to the reversionary element in the other half, on the death of their mother.
- Mr Jones can choose his own personal representatives rather than have them determined under the Non-Contentious Probate Rules. Further, the authority of executors will date from death whereas the authority of administrators dates only from the grant of representation.
- It will be possible to appoint guardians.
- Executors' powers can be varied or extended.
- The making of a will provides an opportunity for tax-planning. Any inheritance tax that might be due on the death of the first of Mr and Mrs Jones to die can be avoided by taking advantage of the surviving spouse exemption, although care needs to be taken to avoid the adverse tax effect of the 'bunching' of estates at the survivor's death.
- Directions may be given as to burial and disposal of the deceased's body.

ii) The inheritance tax position is that none will be payable on the death of Mr Jones in respect of property passing to his wife because of the surviving spouse exemption. And this is so whether the interest he takes is an absolute or life-interest.

iii) An absolute interest would give Mrs Jones access to and freedom to deal with the capital. It follow that there will be no guarantee that Mrs Jones will use what she is left for the benefit of the children. While a life-interest will enable Mr Jones to control the ultimate destination of the capital in his estate it does limit Mrs Jones to the receipt of income only, unless the trustees of his will are given express power to advance capital or even make a loan.

iv) A pension scheme, such as this, allows contributors to 'nominate' a third party to receive benefits after the contributor's death (Mr Jones), either in the form of a lump sum, as here, or a pension. Its relative size is such as to make it potentially a substantial asset, but it is only payable on the death of Mr Jones in service and, therefore, any provision by way of 'nomination' to a beneficiary will need to be reviewed if Mr Jones ceases to contribute to the XYZ Ltd scheme, whether on retirement or because of changing jobs.

Such a benefit will not form part of Mr Jones's estate for inheritance tax purposes and unlike most nominations, strictu senso, this type of 'nomination' is not binding on the trustees of the pension fund but merely an indication of the deceased's wishes (which should, nevertheless, be respected). It would seem sensible tax planning advice to 'nominate' a proportion of the sum in favour of the children by way of contract to any benefits to which they would become entitled under the will (which subject to the nil rate band, would be taxed).

b) The lifetime points that might arise are, first, equalisation of estates; and, secondly, taking advantage of available lifetime exemptions, such as the annual £3,000 to each if the estates are equalised and potentially exempt transfers (PETs). As regards Mrs Jones making a will it would be advisable for her to do so, even though at present her estate is worth very little. If Mr Jones leaves her a life-interest only in his will then she will have no powers of disposition over it. Bearing in mind Mr Jones's clear wish to see the children benefited she should at least make a will complementary to his, leaving, it is suggested, everything to him if he survives by a stated period but otherwise leaving it equally between the children.

Two further points emerge: first, even if Mr Jones dies intestate some of the statutory legacy may be unspent at the time of Mrs Jones's death; and second, Mrs Jones's estate would be increased by the XYZ Ltd pension fund money.

c) i) Standard provisions which should be included in the will are the following:

- Extension of the power to invest beyond the terms of the Trustee Investments Act 1961, so that they can invest as if beneficial owners and therefore so as to include investment in assets which are not income-producing, eg a residence for personal occupation by any of the beneficiaries.

- Variation of the maintenance provisions of s31 Trustee Act 1925 so that it is not necessary to consider the availability of income from other funds and to permit a more subjective test to be applied to determine what is reasonable.
- Extension of the provisions of s32 Trustee Act 1925, which gives power to raise capital and advance up to one-half of the vested or presumptive share for the benefit of a child. Power should be given to advance more than merely one-half.
- Extension of the provisions of s19 Trustee Act 1925, so that insurance can be effected up to the full value of the property against loss or damage by fire or other risks and so that premiums may be payable from capital or income.
- Provision for receipt for income/capital from a minor's parents/guardians, or from minor himself or herself, if over 16. This will enable the trustees to be discharged from the trusts.
- A solicitor's charging clause allowing you or your firm to charge for work done, whether or not in a professional capacity.
- Variation of s41 AEA 1925, by giving power to appropriate assets to a beneficiary without obtaining the required consents. (However, much of the advantage in this, which had been to eliminate ad valorem stamp duty, has been obviated by s84 Finance Act 1985, which has removed such duty on instruments of appropriation.)

ii) One of the reasons for such a conditional gift is that by s184 Law of Property Act 1925, if two or more persons die in circumstances such that there is no evidence as to which died first, then for the purposes of succession to the property the younger is deemed to have survived the elder.

Thus, a gift by the elder to the younger devolves as part of the latter's estate. Section 184 can be excluded by means of a survivorship clause. It is not known who is the elder on the facts of the question.

Another relevant factor concerns tax. Section 184 LPA has no application for the purposes of IHT payable upon death, so that each of those concerned is treated as having died at the same instant. If the elder left property to the younger, it is taxed as part of the elder's estate only.

With regard to an express survivorship provision as here, therefore, provided the survival period is expressed to be not in excess of six months, if death occurs within the period inheritance tax is payable on the death of the first spouse to die but none is payable on the death of the second. In the event of survival for the period there is no tax to pay on the first death (because of the surviving spouse exemption) but tax will be payable on the second death, subject to the nil-rate band.

If there is no survivorship clause no tax will be payable on the death of the first spouse to die (surviving spouse exemption) but, subject again to the nil-rate band, tax will be payable on the death of the second spouse.

A survivorship clause, also has the benefit of vesting 'control' of the ultimate destination of the property in Mr Jones. Administrative convenience is ensured. A further point to consider is what happens if there is a divorce? *Re Sinclair* (1985) (see clause 4 of the will draft as explained in clause 5) allows for this.

iii) The considerations of a succession nature which should be discussed with Mr Jones regarding the proposed gifts to the sons are threefold: first, whether the gifts should be vested or contingent, and if contingent subject to what contingency? Second, whether there is a possibility of further children and if so the advisability of including a generic clause; and thirdly, the desirability of including a substitutional gift to grandchildren or issue rather than relying upon the provisions of s33 Wills Act 1837, as substituted by s19 Administration of Justice Act 1982. It is better practice to make specific provision by way of substitution but in any event the testator may wish to insert an age qualification and/or exclude the entitlement of any illegitimate child (both of which he could only do by inserting a substitutional clause).

d) THIS IS THE LAST WILL AND TESTAMENT of me BILL JONES of 1 KINGS ROAD, ST SAMPSONS

1. I HEREBY REVOKE all Wills Codicils and testamentary dispositions heretofore made by me

2. I APPOINT ABC (ie CANDIDATE) and my brother George Jones (hereinafter called 'my trustees' which expression where the context admits shall include the trustee or trustees hereof for the time being whether original or substituted) to be the executors and trustees hereof and (I DECLARE that any of my trustees being a solicitor or other person engaged in any profession or business shall be entitled to charge and be paid (without abatement) all usual professional or other charges for business done services rendered or time spent by him or his firm in the administration of my estate or the trusts hereof including acts which a trustee not engaged in any profession or business could have done personally).

[3. I APPOINT (names required) to be the guardians after the death of my said wife of any of my children who may then be minors]

4. If my wife HILDA JONES survives me thirty days (but not otherwise) I GIVE to her absolutely (but SUBJECT nevertheless to the payment of my debts and funeral and testamentary expenses) all my estate both real and personal whatsoever and wheresoever

5. If my said wife is not living at my death or does not survive me by thirty days or if the gift in clause 4 shall fail for any reason I GIVE to my trustees all my estate as aforesaid UPON TRUST to sell call in and convert the same into money (with full power to postpone such sale calling in and conversion of all or any part or parts of my estate indefinitely or for so long as in their absolute discretion they may think fit without being liable for loss and notwithstanding that the same may be of a wasting speculative or reversionary nature) and after payment thereout of my debts and funeral and testamentary expenses TO HOLD the balance thereof and all parts of my said estate for the time being unsold and unconverted (hereinafter together called 'my residuary estate') UPON TRUST for all my children living at my death who attain the age of eighteen years and if more than one in equal shares absolutely PROVIDED ALWAYS that if any child of mine shall die in my lifetime leaving a child or children living at my death who attain the age of eighteen years such last mentioned child or children shall take by substitution and if more than one in equal shares the share of my residuary estate which his or her parent would have taken if he or she had survived to attain a vested interest

[6. MY TRUSTEES shall have the following powers in addition to their powers under the general law:]

IN WITNESS whereof I have hereunto set my hand this day of 19

SIGNED by the above-named BILL JONES)
as his last will in the presence of us present)
at the same time who at his request in his)
presence and in the presence of each other)
have hereunto subscribed our names as)
witnesses:)

QUESTION 4

You are a partner in AB & C, solicitors of Bank House, North Town. Your offices are over the local branch of Allbank PLC and the manager there frequently sends his customers to you with instructions for their wills. You have just received one set of such instructions in the form of a letter as follows:

'Allbank PLC
North Town

AB & C — 10th February 1988

Solicitors
Bank House
North Town

Dear Sirs

Will you please prepare a will for our customer George Andrews of Church House, North Town for whom I think you will remember acting when he purchased Church House some four years ago.

Mr Andrews is aged 32. His wife, Hilda, is aged 30. There are two children, Kate and Claire, aged seven and four.

The total value of the estate is about £500,000 of which the house is worth about £100,000, the bulk of the rest being marketable securities.

Please draft a will for Mr Andrews leaving the whole of his estate to his wife absolutely if she survives him by 30 days, subject only to a prior legacy for Kate and Claire of £90,000 (for the usual reason), this to be divided equally between them contingently on their reaching 25.

The executor is to be Allbank Trust Company PLC.

Please send the draft to Mr Brown of out trust company for approval. Subject to any comments he may have, please let me have the engrossment and I will see Mr Andrews and get him to sign it.

Yours sincerely

Manager.'

Note to candidates:

With regard to inheritance tax, you should assume that there have been no potentially exempt or chargeable transfers.

(a) Explain your position as solicitor from the point of view of professional conduct in this case and the steps you would take to discharge your duties in this regard.

6 marks

(b) Explain what you think the bank manager means when referring to the gift to to children as being made 'for the usual reason'.

5 marks

(c) Explain the background to and purpose of the condition that if Mrs Andrews is to take she must survive Mr Andrews by 30 days.

In your answer please deal with the interaction of the spouse exemption from inheritance tax and the condition that Mrs Andrews must survive Mr Andrews by 30 days.

7 marks

(d) What points occur to you about the gift to Kate and Claire? In your answer you should cover any matters on which you consider further instructions may be required and regarding which you would wish to give advice. Please also deal briefly with all relevant tax considerations, except the question of inheritance tax payable at Mr Andrews' death.

16 marks

(e) Allowing for any suggestions you make in your answer to (d) set out in your own words those parts of the draft will dealing with the gift to Mrs Andrews and all other provisions dealing with the gift of the residuary estate.

10 marks

(f) Briefly explaining and giving reasons for them, what administrative provision would you include in your draft of the will?

10 marks

(g) Assume that when the engrossment is ready the bank manager tells you that Mr Andrews has had a sudden heart attack and is in hospital. He therefore asks you to take the engrossment to Mr Andrews at the hospital so that it can be signed there. When you arrive at the hospital Mr Andrews is conscious but close to death. His own doctor, Dr Jones, is with him when you arrive. What special precautions would you take regarding the execution of the will at the hospital and why?

5 marks

---

59 marks

Law Society Solicitors' Final Examination
Wills, Probate and Administration Winter 1988 Q1

QUESTION 4 - SOLUTION

General comment

This question, carrying 59 marks, was divided into seven sub-questions, none of which should have overtaxed the well-prepared student. Question-spotters were well served in that four of the sub-questions had appeared before, in slightly different factual situations, emphasising yet again that after eight years of the current model the examiner, understandably perhaps, is having difficulty in inventing new themes.

Suggested solution

a) From the point of view of professional conduct, the instructions are directed to the firm in the letter, and not to the individual partner concerned. Furthermore, the instructions have not been received from the client George Andrews but from his bank manager. Professional practice ethics requires Andrews himself to instruct the individual solicitor who will be involved in the drawing up of the will and for those instructions to be recorded and discussed with the client. The solicitor should therefore decline to accept the instructions for George Andrews and insist upon an appointment with Andrews himself: unless this is done the solicitor is in breach of his professional ethical duties.

b) The bank manager, when referring to the gift to children being made 'for the usual reason', is alluding to the fact that revenue considerations will be a paramount determinant in the planning of the will. The value of the estate (£500,000) is substantial: it will therefore be advisable to mitigate the impact of inheritance tax as far as possible. Utilising the nil rate band in respect of legacies to non-exempt beneficiaries, (the children, Kate and Claire) can be achieved by leaving £128,000 to the children on the death of the first spouse, this being the nil rate band for the time being in force.

c) The background to, and purpose of, the survivorship period that will require Mrs Andrews to survive Mr Andrews by 30 days should be examined in the context of its consequences, as regards both succession and inheritance tax.

After having considered the possibility of Mrs Andrews dying shortly after him, Mr Andrews will be contemplating the inclusion of a survivorship period for the purpose of retaining control over the destination of his estate and with a view to avoiding the delay and expense of double administration.

The usual 30-day period anticipates not only actual survival by a short period, but also the notional survival which is deemed to occur in the light of s184 Law of Property Act 1925 - that is, that if two or more persons die in circumstances such that there is no evidence as to which was the survivor, then for the purposes of succession to property the younger is deemed to have survived the elder. Accordingly, a gift to the younger - Hilda Andrews - would devolve as part of the latter's estate. So the survival of Mrs Andrews will not enable her personal representatives to claim under the will if she dies within 30 days of George Andrews.

As regards inheritance tax, if the clause is retained and Mrs Andrews survives the required period the transfer to her of her husband's entire estate would be exempt because of the spouse exemption. However, if she survives him only to die within 30 days inheritance tax will be chargeable as if she had acquired no interest in his property: inheritance tax will thus be payable on the death of the first spouse to die but none will be payable on the death of the second spouse.

If the clause is deleted, no inheritance tax will be payable on the death of the first spouse to die because of the spouse exemption but there will be inheritance tax to pay on the death of the second. Whether or not the survivorship clause is retained, if the order of deaths is uncertain both are deemed to die at the same instant: IHT would only be payable on the death of the elder.

d) The gift to Kate and Claire, to share £128,000 between them, will not be a vested gift but will be one contingent upon both attaining 25: if one should do so but not the other then, in the manner intimated in the instructions, the whole legacy would not vest in the survivor but the failed share would lapse into the residue. By making the legacies contingent they will not vest on the testator's death and be payable at 18 (at which date a valid receipt can be given, but not before this age). Is this the testator's true intentions? This should be checked with Mr Andrews.

Mr and Mrs Andrews are a young married couple. They may well have further children. It would be better to make provision of a sum of £128,000 as a generic gift, rather than by name: the date when the class closes should be specified, thereby overriding the class-closing rules - eg 'to all my children living at the date of my death a sum equivalent to the nil-rate band in force for the time being, to be shared equally'.

Consideration, further, should be given to a substitutional gift to grandchildren or issue should a child predecease. The usual provision, in this context, is for a distribution 'per stirpes', the children of a deceased child dividing his share between them, rather than 'per capita'.

The personal representatives will hold the children's interest on trust to await fulfilment of the contingency. The beneficiaries, having a contingent right to capital, can, by virtue of s31 Trustee Act 1925, require the income generated by the capital to be accumulated in so far as it is not applied for maintenance, education or benefit: in practice, the trustees will do this anyway.

While the children's interest in income is contingent the trustees are liable at basic rate and additional rate on the gross amount of the trust income. Only the gross equivalent of sums actually paid for maintenance, education or benefit will enter the children's statutory income: these sums will be grossed-up at basic and additional rates. Thus, income which is accumulated does not enter the beneficiary's statutory income: if income is applied and does, therefore, enter statutory income, the beneficiary will receive a tax deduction certificate showing the tax paid by the trustees on his behalf.

A notable tax consideration is placing the children's entitlement on an accumulations and maintenance settlement. This would satisfy the requirements of s71 Inheritance Tax Act 1984, provided: no interest in possession at the inception of the trust (ie present right to enjoyment of the income); all the beneficiaries trace ancestry through a common grandparent (clearly they do); one or more of the beneficiaries attains an interest in possession in the settled property on or before attaining 25. Entitlement to income at 18 under s31 Trustee Act 1925 will give an interest in possession. The effect of such an accumulations and maintenance settlement will be that although there is a charge to tax on the creation of the settlement, there is no periodic charge to tax every tenth year and no 'exit' charge at the termination of the settlement.

e) Those parts of the draft will dealing with the gift to Mrs Andrews and all other provisions dealing with the gift of the residuary estate would appear as hereunder:

(4) If my said wife survives me by 30 days (but not otherwise) I GIVE to her absolutely (but subject nevertheless to the payment of my debts and funeral and testamentary expenses) all my estate both real and personal whatsoever and wheresoever.

(5) If my said wife is not living at my death or does not survive me by thirty days (but not otherwise) I GIVE to my trustees all my estate as aforesaid UPON TRUST to sell call in and convert the same into money (with full power to postpone such sale calling in and conversion of all or any part or parts of my estate indefinitely or for so long as in their absolute discretion they may think fit without being liable for loss and notwithstanding that the same may be of a wasting, speculative or reversionary nature) and after payment thereout of my debts and funeral and testamentary expenses to hold the balance thereof and all parts of my said estate for the time being unsold and unconverted (hereafter together called 'my residuary estate') UPON TRUST for all my children living at my death who attain the age of eighteen years or earlier marry and if more than one in equal shares absolutely PROVIDED ALWAYS that if any child of mine shall die in my lifetime leaving a child or children living at my death who attain the age of eighteen years or marry under that age such last mentioned child or children shall take by substitution and if more than one in equal shares the share of my residuary estate which his/her or their parent would have taken if he or she had survived to attain a vested interest.

f) The administrative provisions for inclusion in the draft of the will would be as follows:

i) Extension of the power to invest beyond the terms of the Trustee Investments Act 1961 so that the trustees can invest as if beneficial owners and therefore so as to include investment in assets which are not income - producing, eg a residence for personal occupation by any of the beneficiaries.

ii) Variation of the maintenance provisions of s31 Trustee Act 1925 so that it is not necessary to consider the availability of income from other funds and to permit a more subjective test to be applied to determine what is reasonable.

iii) Extension of the provisions of s32 Trustee Act 1925, which gives power to raise capital and advance up to one-half of the vested or presumptive share for the benefit of a child. Power should be given to advance more than merely one-half.

iv) Extension of the provisions of s19 Trustee Act 1925, so that insurance can be effected up to the full value of the property against loss or damage by fire or other risks and so that premiums may be payable from capital or income.

v) Provision for receipt for income/capital from a minor's parents/guardians, or from the minor himself or herself, if over 16. This will enable the trustees to be discharged from the trusts.

vi) A solicitor's charging clause allowing the firm ABC, solicitors, to charge for work done, whether or not in a professional capacity: such a charging clause could be in accordance with *Re Horgan* (1971).

vii) Variation of s41 Administration of Estates Act 1925, by giving power to appropriate assets to a beneficiary without obtaining the required consents. Much of this advantage, however, which had been to eliminate ad valorem stamp duty, has been obviated by s84 Finance Act 1985, which has removed such duty on instruments of appropriation.

g) It will be necessary to ascertain that Mr Andrews has capacity to make the will. In *Kenward* v *Adams* (1975), Templeman J advised solicitors acting for elderly or infirm testators (and here Mr Andrews is clearly infirm although not elderly) to consult with the testator's nearest relatives before drawing up his will and to ensure that at least one of the witnesses was medically qualified and prepared to record at the time of execution his satisfaction with the testator's capacity and understanding. Dr Jones should be asked to record these matters and should, it is suggested, be asked to witness the will. Because of the solicitor's charging clause no solicitor of the firm should witness the will.

A further precaution is that the attestation clause should be altered to show that the will was read over to Mr Andrews and that he appeared fully to understand its contents.

Templeman J, further, in *Re Simpson* (1977) declared: 'The will ought to be witnessed and approved by a medical practitioner who satisfies himself as to the capacity and understanding of the testator and makes a record of his examination and findings. I hope the Law Society will consider whether sufficient guidance is given to students and practitioners'.

A careful and full file note should be made.

QUESTION 5

Simon Coke (aged 40) is a director of a large public company. He is married to Elsie (35). They have four children aged respectively 14, eight, seven and five. Both Simon and Elsie enjoy good health.

Simon wishes to make a will, besides seeking general tax advice. Simon and Elsie wish as their priority to ensure that if Simon dies before Elsie she will be properly provided for, but they also wish to make appropriate provision for the children.

Simon explains that Elsie is not in paid employment. As they consider that she effectively has no assets they have given no thought to her making a will.

The following are the main family property interests:

Description		Total Estimated value £
A. The matrimonial home (Greenacre), owned by Simon subject to a mortgage to the Blankshire Building Society	400,000 150,000	250,000
B. Policies of assurance on Simon's life, payable to his personal representatives		100,000
C. Death in service lump sum under the pension scheme of Simon's company, amounting to twice his pay at date of death. (This sum is payable to Simon's dependants at the trustees' discretion. Simon has not indicated hiswishes to the trustees.)		80,000
D. Bank and building society accounts:	Simon	60,000
	Elsie	2,000
E. Simon's life interest under the will of his father, who died in August 1986. (The remaindermen are defined as those of Simon's children who were alive at his father's death.) The trust fund is primarily a substantial holding in the shares of B & C Ltd, an unquoted company which does not pay dividends. The company has good prospects. The trust fund is valued at		300,000
F. Simon's 30 per cent holding is a new private company, Style Ltd, which he believes has excellent long-term prospects		1,000

G. Trust fund settled by Elsie's grandmother on trust for Olive for life, remainder to Elsie. Olive (63) is in good health and says the trust income is not essential to her requirements. The trust fund is valued at 60,000

Neither Simon nor Elsie has made any lifetime gifts.

Advise Simon and Elsie:

a) Whether Elsie should take any action now, and if so what, to mitigate inheritance tax should she die unexpectedly. You should deal in particular with her reversionary interest, explaining the inheritance tax reasons for any recommendations you make.

11 marks Your advice should include any steps which Olive might consider.

b) What provision could be made by Simon for Elsie and the children, without reducing Simon's current income, whether this is to take effect now or upon his death.

You should consider the tax planning potential of each item listed in the question separately and set out in each case the likely capital tax implications.

Should the creation of a beneficial joint tenancy or tenancy in common in respect of any of the items appears to you to be worthwhile, as a matter of tax planning or convenience for the surviving spouse, you should include this in your recommendations covering that item. **17 marks**

c) Whether Elsie should in fact make a will. Do not set out its provisions. **4 marks**

---

32 marks

Law Society Solicitors' Final Examination
Wills, Probate and Administration Summer 1988 Q2

QUESTION 5 - SOLUTION

General comment

Carrying nearly one-third of the marks, this question was for the greater part an exercise in tax planning. It was very testing for most students and must have come as something of a surprise.

Nevertheless it was perfectly fair and will have had the merit of separating the wheat from the chaff (which is not always achieved in question-setting). A candidate with less than detailed knowledge of inheritance tax planning can expect to have done badly.

Suggested solution

a) As the position stands at present Elsie has assets which are within the nil-rate band of £128,000 and therefore if she should die unexpectedly, before her husband, it does not appear that any inheritance tax would be payable. Furthermore, under the provisions of any will Elsie might make, or intestacy, her property would be spouse exempt in so far as it passed to her husband.

The basic charge to inheritance tax on death arises on the aggregate of a person's 'estate' immediately before their death, a liability which may be increased by any potentially exempt transfers (PETs) which become chargeable.

Excluded property does not form part of the owner's estate on death for inheritance tax purposes and within the category of 'excluded property' is Elsie's reversionary interest in the trust fund settled by Elsie's grandmother on Olive for life, with remainder to Elsie. It would only be taxable if acquired for money or money's worth, or vested in the settlor or settlor's spouse, neither of which condition applies here.

If Olive should predecease Elsie the trustees will transfer the fund to Elsie and if Olive's death estate contains other aggregable assets the trust fund is likely to suffer inheritance tax at her death. Elsie will receive the trust fund diminished by such inheritance tax as is payable according to the scale rates.

Olive could contemplate surrendering her life-interest immediately or in the very near future: the effect would be to accelerate Elsie's interest so that she would get the fund now. It would be a PET by Olive. Elsie, on receipt of the fund, could then transfer it to her children. This would also be a PET.

If Olive does nothing Elsie could always make a settlement of her interest in remainder for the benefit of her children and if she does so the trust fund will pass to them directly on the death of Olive. There will be no PET by Elsie where, for example, she survives Olive only for a short time nor would there be aggregation of the trust fund assets in her 'death estate' in that event.

b) Provision that could be made by Simon for Elsie and the children without reducing Simon's current income is considered here in the context of each available asset.

i) *Greenacre*

At present Simon is sole owner. Elsie should be made a beneficial co-owner, joint-tenancy being perhaps preferable to a tenancy in common in that the surviving spouse will take by accretion. Under a beneficial joint tenancy a survivorship clause is not possible: if a tenancy in common is preferred, provided both make a will a survivorship clause and a gift-over are then possible. Either spouse might contemplate giving their shares to their children direct by will.

Greenacre is a substantial asset and Simon should arrange mortgage protection cover in regard to the charge in favour of Blankshire Building Society.

ii) *Policies of assurance on Simon's life*

At present the policies will form part of Simon's estate and will be chargeable to inheritance tax if the spouse exemption does not apply. He could take the policies out of his estate by assigning the benefits direct to his children if he and Elsie feel she would otherwise be adequately provided for.

iii) *Lump sum*

As this sum is payable to Simon's dependants at the trustees' discretion it is already outside the estate for inheritance tax purposes. Simon could write to the trustees asking them to consider paying half to the children and half to Elsie, paying her more than half should her needs at his death so require.

iv) *Bank and building society accounts*

As these will be income-producing assets they should be left as they are. For the sake of convenience they could all be put into joint-names and the survivor could then draw on them before probate.

v) *Life interest*

Simon could surrender his life interest by effecting an instrument of variation, his father having died under two years ago. As regards inheritance tax, there will be no extra charge to tax, or if he fails to survive the variation by seven years, because the variation will be treated as having been made under the will.

Alternatively, Simon could make a PET. If he died within seven years the chargeable transfer would be the value of the fund at the date of the transfer, net of any business property relief. Thus, the anticipated growth in the fund would not be charged upon his death within seven years.

So far as capital gains tax is concerned, there would be none chargeable if he and the trustees agree to hold over the gain, although there could be CGT on a sale of shares.

vi) *Simon's 30 per cent holding in Style Ltd, valued at £1,000*

Simon could settle his shares on the children. The value is small and falls within the inheritance tax annual exemption, which is relevant if Simon dies within seven years: it would also be exempt as a transfer for the children's maintenance. Further, the post-settlement growth in the value of the shares would be outside Simon's estate, even if he were to die within seven years.

In relation to capital gains tax it would seem better not to exercise hold-over relief if any gain on transfer falls within Simon's annual exemption. This will give the children's trustees a higher base value for the shares, assuming they are now worth more than what he paid for them.

c) Elsie should make a will for a number of reasons.

Elsie is likely to receive considerable assets, especially if Simon predeceases her. In view of the children's ages it is important for the personal representatives and guardians to be chosen by the parents, should both die while the children are still minors: it is equally important that they be given wide powers.

Other reasons, in general terms, for Elsie making a will are: to effect dispositions as a conscious exercise rather than relying on the intestacy rules; to show a positive demonstration of generosity, perhaps in favour of a charity or a retainer; to extend the somewhat restrictive statutory powers of executors; taxation planning considerations, utilising reliefs and exemptions; peace of mind.

QUESTION 6

As an assistant solicitor with ABC Solicitors of Southtown you are consulted by Herbert and Joan Green of 1 Northside, Southtown, about their making wills.

Joan has had considerable difficulty in persuading Herbert to do this. His attitude has always been 'It will all go to you (meaning Joan) and then to the children equally and that is what I want, so why bother and pay the solicitors for nothing'.

Eventually Joan draws attention to the advertisement your firm has published in the local press 'Wills on the cheap - from as little as £5.00 a time and free if you appoint us executors'. She also points out that they have always agreed that if the family (consisting of Herbert (aged 55), Joan (35) and two children (seven and five) were all killed in a common calamity, everything should go to XYZ a local charity.

Herbert was previously married to Angela Green by whom there were no children. At the time of their divorce and as part of the matrimonial proceedings various capital adjustments were made between the parties. These resulted in Angela purchasing Herbert's share in the then matrimonial home. No provision was made for periodic payments. However, occasionally Angela has sought help from Herbert in order to supplement her income; this he has always provided, albeit on an entirely voluntary basis.

The value of Herbert's estate is currently about £150,000. The matrimonial home, which is in his name only, accounts for £75,000, personal chattels for about £2,000 and the remainder is made up of bank and building society deposits and a few investments in unit trusts.

Joan has almost nothing of her own; just £2,000 on deposit with a bank, which she would like to go to the children.

(Note to candidates:

(i) Finance Act 1989 provides for inheritance tax to be charged at a single rate of 40 per cent on all transfers not within the nil rate band of £118,000.

(ii) Assume that the clients have not made any lifetime gifts.)

14 marks (a) Advise generally whether Herbert and also Joan should indeed bother to make wills. Explain how their wishes could be put into effect. You should contrast what you suggest with what would happen if either died intestate. To what extent, if any, do you consider inheritance tax to be relevant? State briefly whether any charge to inheritance tax might be alleviated by action taken inter vivos.

8 marks (b) Explain the advice, if any, you would give regarding Angela.

5 marks (c) Give and explain your opinion of the advertisement which your firm has placed in the local press.

(d) What information will you require to draft the gift to the charity? What special provisions should you make in drafting such a gift?

If because of faulty drafting the gift to the charity is invalid what action, if any, may the charity take?

7 marks

(e) On the basis of the advice you give to Herbert concerning his will, set out in your own words a draft of the will you suggest, appointing your firm as executors. There is no need to follow any particular precedent as long as what is proposed is clear and effective.

23 marks

57 marks

Law Society Solicitors' Final Examination
Wills, Probate and Administration Winter 1989 Q1

QUESTION 6 - SOLUTION

General comment

This was a fairly standard pre-death question and the main issues have been asked several times before. As a slight variation there were questions on professional practice and drafting gifts to a charity. The question should have posed no problems to a reasonably well prepared student.

Suggested solution

a) It is not completely clear what Herbert means when he says 'It will all go to Joan and then to the children equally.' It is unlikely that as a layman he intends a life interest to Joan and he probably has a vague idea that the property will go to Joan on his death and then to the children on her death without any precise or clear notion of how this is to be achieved. The first step should be to inform him of how the intestacy rules would operate if he failed to make a will.

If Herbert dies intestate, Joan would inherit all the personal chattels absolutely, a legacy of £75,000 and a life interest in one-half of the residue of the estate. She would be able to elect to have the matrimonial home appropriated to her in or towards satisfaction of her absolute interest in the estate and also to capitalise her life interest. The remainder interest in that half of the residue would go to the children contingent on attaining the age of 18 and the other half of the residue would pass to the children immediately again contingent on attaining the age of 18.

On the facts of this problem this distribution may well be unsatisfactory. Herbert sounds as though he does not wish his children to inherit until after Joan's death and the provision made for Joan under the intestacy rules could well be inadequate. On current values if she exercised her rights in relation to the matrimonial home, this would exhaust her statutory legacy and her remaining share of the estate might not produce an adequate income for her. If Herbert died in a few years time after property prices had increased, the position would be even worse.

If Joan died intestate before Herbert, he would inherit all her small estate. If both spouses were to die, the joint estates would pass to the children. There is no way of ensuring that the joint estates pass to the XYZ charity if the family is killed in a common accident unless wills are made.

Apart from the distribution of the property, there are other reasons in this case for recommending the making of wills. The children are both young and Herbert and Joan should consider the appointment of testamentary guardians for them. In addition they could use wills to appoint executors, grant wider administrative powers to the executors and make any small gifts of sentimental value.

If a will is made, there are three main options for Herbert to consider. He could leave all his estate to Joan, subject to her surviving him by a short period (say 30 days), and otherwise to the children. If he failed to include the survivorship clause, his estate might pass to her although both died together and she was only deemed to survive him under s184 LPA 1925, or she did survive him by a very short period. Thus, he retains greater control over the disposition of his property. The main disadvantage of this proposal is that there is no guarantee that the property will pass to the children if Joan survives Herbert.

His second main option is to divide his estate in some proportions between Joan and the children. This has the obvious advantage of ensuring that part, at least, of the property does pass to the children in any event. The disadvantage is that a division may leave Joan inadequately provided for, and this is particularly important in view of her age. If Herbert dies in the next ten years, Joan could have a long widowhood. A further disadvantage is that if Herbert dies while the children are still under 18, their share would have to be held on trust for them, which would involve extra trouble and expense.

The third option is to leave the estate on trust for Joan for her life with remainder to the children and perhaps an outright legacy to Joan of part of the estate. This would again ensure that the children inherited on Joan's death, but there would be the disadvantages of the trouble and expense of maintaining the trust and the possibility that Joan might not be properly provided for unless the trust contained a power for the trustees to pay capital sums to her.

If Joan were to die before Herbert, her small estate would pass to him and her stated wish is for it to pass to the children. She must make a will in order to effect this. She should also consider the possibility that she dies after Herbert and having inherited under his will. If at that time the children were still minors, it would be important that there was a properly drafted will to grant the children's trustees the necessary administrative powers.

If Herbert dies intestate before Joan, that part of his estate which passes to her will be exempt from tax and the part which passes to the children will be within the nil rate band. On Joan's death, if her estate then passes to the children, there will be a potential tax charge, although on current values her estate would not be over the nil rate band (as part of Herbert's estate would already have passed to the children). If Joan dies first, there would be no tax on her death but there would be tax on Herbert's death.

If wills are made and Herbert leaves all his estate to Joan there would be no tax on his death but tax would be due on Joan's death. She would have the opportunity of making lifetime gifts to the children which would be potentially exempt transfers. One advantage of leaving part of Herbert's estate direct to the children would be to utilise his nil rate band and thus reduce the total tax bill. The tax advantage would have to be compared to the other disadvantages of this course. There would be no tax advantage of leaving his estate on trust for Joan for life with remainder to the children as it would be taxed in full on Joan's death.

In this type of case it is suggested that in spite of the apparent tax disadvantages, it is probably preferable to leave Herbert's estate to Joan absolutely to ensure that she is properly provided for. If she finds that she does not need all the money, she can make lifetime gifts to the children free of tax, if she survives for seven years.

One problem here is that while Herbert's estate is above the nil rate band, Joan's is well within it. If Herbert and Joan were to die together in a common accident, there is a potential tax bill on Herbert's estate. If the joint assets were more equally divided this could be avoided as both estates would be within the nil rate limits. Thus, it is suggested that either some assets are transferred to the name of Joan, or some assets are placed in joint names in order to bring Herbert's assets within the nil rate limit. The house could be put into joint names and some of the deposit accounts. This would have the additional advantage of ensuring Joan was not temporarily short of money if Herbert died first. This measure will not make any difference for tax purposes if one spouse dies some time before the other. The jointly owned property would pass by survivorship to the other spouse and be tax free.

b) As Herbert's ex-spouse Angela would have no claim on his intestacy, and he can exclude her from his will, but she may have a potential claim under the Inheritance Act 1975. If the divorce settlement contained a court order barring her from such a claim, or she has re-married, she could not claim. If her claim is not barred, is it likely to succeed? In *Re Fullard* (1982) the Court of Appeal indicated that claims by an ex-spouse were not likely to succeed if there had been a full settlement on the divorce unless the death caused a change in financial circumstances, by bringing periodical payments to an end or making further capital available. In this case Herbert has been assisting Angela financially on a voluntary basis. Whether Angela could make a successful claim depends partly on her own circumstances on Herbert's death and partly on how frequently and to what extent he has been helping her. Broadly, one can say that the greater the degree of help and the more frequent it was, the more likely her claim is to succeed. Herbert could leave a statement setting out why he has made no provision for Angela on his death, explaining that there had been a final settlement on the divorce and that his later assistance was purely voluntary. Such a statement would be considered by the court but would not be conclusive as the test is not whether Herbert acted reasonably, but whether reasonable financial provision was made for Angela. It is suggested that he makes it clear to Angela, if he is asked to help her in the future, that he does not intend to provide for her on his death and that any help he does give is purely voluntary and may not continue indefinitely. From the point of view of defeating any family provision claim, it might be best to cease helping Angela at all, but that might be unacceptable on other grounds.

c) The advertisement may well be in breach of the Solicitors' Publicity Code. It is prohibited by the Code to state a fee as being from or upwards of a certain figure and, while publicity may state that a particular service is free of charge, this may not be conditional on the solicitor being given any other instructions in connection with that or any other matter. Thus, the advertisement appears to breach the Code in two respects. Generally, any publicity must be in good taste. The Council encourages local law societies to bring less serious breaches to the attention of the solicitors concerned but persistent or serious cases would be reported to the Solicitors' Complaints Bureau.

d) Care should be taken to ensure that the correct name of the charity is quoted in the will to avoid any doubt as to which institution is to benefit. The current Charities Digest should be checked. This will also ensure that the institution is indeed charitable, which is important as if it is not, problems of non- charitable purpose trusts will arise and laymen often do not appreciate which organisations are charitable in law, so Herbert and Joan could believe wrongly that XYZ is a charity. The will should be drafted to avoid failure of the gift in the event of any change of name or objects, amalgamation or dissolution of the institution.

The will should provide for the executors to be discharged by the receipt of the treasurer or other officer of the institution, so that there is no obligation on the executors to see to the correct application of the gift.

If the gift to the charity failed because of faulty drafting, the charity might be able to apply for rectification of the will. This would only be possible if there had been a clerical error or the draftsman had failed to understand his instructions correctly, for example, if he mistakenly inserted the name of a different charity. If the failure was due to faulty drafting in some other way, the charity might be able to sue the solicitors in negligence on the ground that the draftsman owes a duty of care to the intended beneficiary. In *Ross* v *Caunters* (1980) solicitors were held liable when they failed to warn of the danger of a beneficiary witnessing the will and the principles of that decision might be extended to this type of case.

e) THIS IS THE LAST WILL AND TESTAMENT of me HERBERT GREEN of 1 Northside Southtown

1 I REVOKE all former wills and testamentary dispositions

2 I APPOINT the partners at the date of my death in the firm of ABC of (address required) Southtown or the firm which at the date of my death had succeeded to and carries on its practice to be executors and trustees of this my will (hereinafter called

'my trustees' which expression where the context admits shall include the trustees or trustee hereof for the time being) and I EXPRESS the wish that two and only two of them shall prove my will and act initially in its trusts and I DECLARE that any of my trustees being a solicitor or other person engaged in any profession or business shall be entitled to charge for business done services rendered or time spent by him or his firm in the administration of my estate or the trusts hereof including acts which a trustee not engaged in any profession or business could have done personally

3 I APPOINT (names required) to be the guardians after the death of my wife Joan Green of any of my children who may then be minors

4 If my wife Joan Green survives me by thirty days (but not otherwise) I GIVE to her absolutely (but subject nevertheless to the payment of my debts and funeral and testamentary expenses) all my estate both real and personal whatsoever and wheresoever

5 If my said wife is not living at my death or does not survive me by thirty days or if the gift in clause 4 shall fail for any reason I GIVE to my trustees all my estate as aforesaid UPON TRUST to sell call in and convert the same into money (with full power to postpone such sale calling in and conversion of all or any part or parts of my estate indefinitely or for so long as in their absolute discretion they may think fit without being liable for loss and notwithstanding that the same may be of a wasting speculative or reversionary nature) and after payment thereout of my debts and funeral and testamentary expenses TO HOLD the balance thereof and all parts of my said estate for the time being unsold and unconverted (hereinafter together called 'my residuary estate') UPON TRUST for all my children living at my death who attain the age of eighteen years and if more than one in equal shares absolutely PROVIDED ALWAYS that if any child of mine shall die in my lifetime or shall die after my death but before attaining a vested interest in my residuary estate leaving a child or children who attain the age of eighteen years such last mentioned child or children shall take by substitution and if more than one in equal shares the share of my residuary estate which his or her or their parent would have taken if he or she had survived to attain a vested interest

6 If the gifts in clauses 4 and 5 should both fail for any reason I GIVE (all my estate as aforesaid) to XYZ (check name) of (address required) absolutely for its general charitable purposes and with full power to expend capital for such purposes and so that my trustees shall not be concerned to see to the application thereof all my estate both real and personal whatsoever and wheresoever (but subject nevertheless to the payment of my debts and funeral and testamentary expenses) AND I DECLARE that the receipt of the person appearing or professing to be the Treasurer or other proper officer for the time being of XYZ shall be a sufficient discharge to my trustees AND I FURTHER DECLARE that if XYZ has changed its name or amalgamated with or transferred its assets to any other body then my trustees shall give effect to the gift as if it had been made (in the first case) to the body in its changed name or (in the second case) to the body which results from such amalgamation or to which the transfer has been made

7 MY TRUSTEES shall have the following powers in addition to their powers under the general law

(1) In their absolute discretion at any time and from time to time to raise capital by way of advancement to any extent (not exceeding the expectant or presumptive share of any particular individual) for any one or more of the following purposes

i) to pay or apply it for the benefit of any one or more of my children or of the children of any of my children who may then have died

ii) to lend it to any one or more of my children without charging interest or taking security and on such terms as to repayment and otherwise as in their absolute discretion (without being liable for loss) my trustees may think fit

(2) To exercise the power of appropriation conferred by s41 of the Administration of Estates Act 1925 without obtaining any of the consents required by that section and even though one or more of them may be beneficially interested

(3) To invest trust money and transpose investments with the same full and unrestricted freedom in their choice of investments as if they were an absolute beneficial owner and to apply trust money at any time and from time to time in the purchase with vacant possession (upon trust for sale with full power to postpone sale) or in the improvement or repair of any freehold or leasehold house or other dwelling and to permit the same to be used as a residence by any person or persons having an interest or prospective interest in my residuary estate upon such terms and conditions from time to time as my trustees in their absolute discretion may think fit

(4) To insure against loss or damage by fire or from any other risk any property for the time being comprised in my residuary estate to any amount and even though a person is absolutely entitled to the property and to pay all premiums for any such insurance at their discretion out of the income or capital of my residuary estate or the property itself and so that any money received under such insurance may be used at their discretion either towards making good the loss or damage in respect of which it was received or as if it were proceeds of sale of the insured property

(5) In any case where they have an obligation or a discretion under the provisions of this my will or under the general law to pay income or capital to or for the benefit of a minor to discharge that obligation or to exercise that discretion if they think fit by making payment either to a parent or guardian of the minor or to the minor personally if of the age of sixteen at least and so that their respective receipts shall be a full discharge to my trustees who shall not be required to see to the application of any income or capital so paid

IN WITNESS whereof I have hereunto set my hand this day of 1989

SIGNED by the above-named HERBERT GREEN)
as his last will in the presence of us present at the)
same time who at his request in his presence and)
in the presence of each other have hereunto)
subscribed our names as witnesses:)

PART TWO
POST-DEATH

5 THE GRANT

5.1 Introduction

The deceased's estate can not be distributed until a grant is obtained. If personal representatives (PRs) have been appointed by will, they are known as executors and the grant will be a grant of probate. If no personal representatives have been appointed, the PRs are administrators and the grant will be letters of administration (with the will annexed, if one exists).

5.2 Key points

a) *General*

i) Responsibility of the solicitor instructed by the intended PRs

Advisory - the solicitor must advise on the beneficial entitlements, on possible claims under family legislation (see chapter 3) and on taxation.

Executive - the solicitor must take all the necessary steps, promptly and efficiently, to extract the appropriate grant, to wind up the estate and to distribute the assets.

Beneficial interests - the solicitor must advise on the possibility and desirability of interim provision.

ii) The distinctions between executors and administrators

Executors can act from death because their authority is derived from the will (the grant simply confirms and relates back to the date of death); administrators cannot act until the issue of the grant because their authority is derived from it.

Administrators can renounce; executors cannot renounce if they act before the grant as this constitutes acceptance.

Infants and persons of unsound mind cannot act as either executors or administrators.

Probate can issue to a sole executor; administration will not generally issue to less than two persons if a minority or life interest arises.

Neither probate nor administration will issue to more than four persons. In probate, power will be reserved to the others.

iii) Procedure for obtaining the grant

Obtain the will, if any.

Ascertain whether the will is admissible to probate:

- Is it the last will of the testator which has not been revoked?
- Has it been validly executed (see chapter 1)?

(NB Probate may be granted of a copy or a draft or a reconstruction of the will, where the will has been lost or accidentally destroyed, provided that it is established by affidavit that:

- the will existed after the death of the testator or was not revoked by destruction;
- the copy/draft/reconstruction is accurate; and
- the will was duly executed.)

Lodge at the Probate Registry (either the Principal Registry of the Family Division of the High Court or the District Probate Registry):

- The will and codicils, if any, duly marked.
- An oath, sworn by the PRs and exhibiting the will, if any, and any renunciation of the executors.
- The Inland Revenue account (if required), signed by the PRs and bearing self-assessment to IHT.
- District Registry - cheque for IHT.

  Principal Registry - receipted Inland Revenue account.
- Probate court fees.
- Request for office copies.

The Registrar may either issue the grant (with office copies, as requested), refuse the grant, request further information or refer it to the judge.

iv) Effect of the grant

Normally, the form is 'general' - all of the estate which by law devolves on and vests in the PRs of the deceased. Any settled land vested in the deceased will generally be excepted from the grant if the land remains settled after death. The land vests in the trustees of the settlement, not the deceased's PRs.

- Grant of probate - confirms the executors' authority and is conclusive evidence of the executors' title and of the validity and the contents of the will.
- Letters of administration - confers authority on the administrators and vests the deceased's property in them. It is conclusive evidence of their title (but not retrospectively).

b) *Administrators*

i) Where a will is in existence, but no executors have been appointed.

The order of priority of administrators is (from the top):

- Residuary trustees.
- Residuary legatees/devisees, whether entitled absolutely, for life or on partial intestacy.
- PRs of residuary legatees/devisees entitled absolutely, or PRs of person(s) entitled on partial intestacy.
- Any other legatees/devisees including those entitled for life or as a trustee, or any creditor.
- PRs of any other legatees/devisees entitled absolutely, or of any creditor.

An applicant with a vested interest is preferred to one who is contingently entitled.

A person in a prior category must either be dead, have renounced or have been cited and failed to make an appearance, before a person in a later category will be entitled to act as administrator ('clearing off').

ii) Where there is no will - total intestacy

The order of priority of administrators is (from the top):

- Spouse of deceased.
- Children and issue of children who have predeceased.
- Parents.
- Brothers and sisters of the whole blood and issue of those who have predeceased.
- Brothers and sisters of the half blood and issue of those who have predeceased.
- Grandparents.
- Uncles and aunts of the whole of the whole blood and issue of those who have predeceased.
- Uncles and aunts of the half-blood and issue of those who have predeceased.
- The Treasury Solicitor on behalf of the Crown. Any creditor or person who would have been entitled if the estate had been larger.

If any of the persons listed above die after the intestate, their PRs have the same right to the grant. However, any living beneficiary is preferred to the PRs of the spouse unless the spouse was beneficially entitled to the whole estate.

iii) Minors

If other adult administrators are entitled in the same degree, the grant will be made to them. If there are none, the letters of administration will be granted for the use and benefit of the minor.

c) *Executors*

The executors are solely entitled to the grant if they are appointed (expressly or by implication) by the will. The rights of executorship cease where the appointed executor:

i) survives the testator but dies before taking out a grant; or

ii) is cited to take out a grant but does not appear to the citation; or

iii) renounces probate.

Minors - minors cannot act as executors nor obtain a grant. If a minor is the sole executor, then:

i) if he has no interest in the residuary estate, the grant will go to those who are entitled to the residuary estate.

ii) if he has an interest in the residuary estate, administration with the will annexed for his use and benefit until he is 18 will be granted (generally to his parents or guardian). When he reaches 18, this will expire and he will be entitled to his own cessate grant.

If he is not the sole executor, probate will be granted to those who are not under a disability and power will be reserved to the minor on attaining 18. When he is 18, there will be a grant of double probate.

d) *Oaths*

The oath is the formal application for the grant by the intended PRs. The oath will comprise of one of three standard forms - Oath for Executors; Oath for Administrators; Oath for Administrators with will.

i) Points common to all oaths

- The time and proper name of the deceased must be given. This will generally be taken from the birth certificate, but if the name has been changed (by marriage/deed poll/habit and repute) the new name should be given with reference to the previous name and explanation at the end of the oath (or in a separate affidavit) of the discrepancy.

- Oaths are generally sworn. However, if the PRs wish to affirm instead, the words 'make oath and say' should be replaced with the words 'do solemnly and sincerely affirm', and the words 'sworn by' should be replaced with 'affirmed by'.

- If the deceased's address at death was different to that in the will, the words 'his only and permanent address' should be deleted and replaced with 'formerly of' and the previous address should be added.
- If the date of death is uncertain, the words 'who was known to be alive on _____ and whose dead body was found on _____' should be used and completed appropriately. If no body has been found, leave should be obtained from the Family Division to swear that the death occurred 'on or since the ___ day of ______ 19___.'
- If the deceased's age is not known, the best possible estimate should be given.
- Settled land (which was settled before the deceased's death and remains settled). If there is none, the relevant paragraph should be left unamended. If settled land does form part of the deceased's estate, the word 'no' should be deleted *and*:

  if the trustees of the settled land are *not the PRs* of the deceased, the words 'save and except settled land' should be inserted at (16);

  if the trustees of the settled land *are the PRs* of the deceased, the words 'including settled land' should be inserted at (16).
- The 'gross estate' includes only property which vests in the PRs. It, therefore, does not include:

  property in which the deceased had a life interest; *or*

  joint property which devolves according to the rules of survivorship; *or*

  property which is the subject of a DMC; *or*

  nominated property.

  The 'net estate' is the gross estate minus debts and liabilities.
- Inland Revenue account (see post). If one is not required, the second paragraph should be deleted and the first paragraph should be completed. If one is required, the reverse should be done.

ii) Points on the oath for executors

- If the time and proper name of the executor is different from that given in the will, the discrepancy should be explained.
- If the executor was appointed by reference to a relationship to the deceased, rather than by name, this relationship should be stated after the executor's name.
- The executor's private address should be given unless he is a professional, administering the estate in his professional capacity.
- The executor's occupation should be given. If the executor has none and is a woman, her marital status should be stated.

- If the original will is not available, the word 'original' should be deleted. If an official copy is available, the words 'as contained in a true and official copy thereof' should be added.
- Power must be reserved to any non-proving or incapacitated executors and notice of the application must be given to them.
- The will and any codicils must be marked and exhibited. The Registrar may require a typed copy if:

  the original is not suitable for copying; *or*

  the original contains alterations which are not suitable for copying; *or*

  the original contains pencil writing. If a copy is made, the words in pencil will be underlined in red; *or*

  the original contains irrelevant matter such as abusive words. The copy will omit them.

iii) Points on the oath for administrators with will

- Persons with prior rights to the grant must be 'cleared off'; it must be stated why the persons with prior rights are not seeking the grant (are dead/have renounced/have failed to appear to a citation). If no executors were appointed in the will, this should be stated.
- The deponent must state the capacity in which he claims the grant.

iv) Points on the oath for administrators

- Persons with prior rights to the grant must be 'cleared off'.
- The deponent must state his relationship to the deceased.

e) *Inland Revenue account*

i) General

PRs must deliver an account to the Revenue within 12 months of the end of the month of death of all the property which formed part of the deceased's estate immediately before death. Delivery is necessary before the grant will be issued.

Interest on unpaid inheritance tax (IHT) runs after six months after the end of the month of death.

The value of the assets and liabilities for IHT purposes are:

- estimated by the PRs and later agreed with the Capital Taxes Office if the valuation is relevant to tax liability; *or*
- negotiated with the Capital Taxes Office or the District Valuer by a professional valuer.

No account needs to be delivered (unless the Revenue specifically request in writing to the PRs within 35 days of the issue of the grant) where:

- The gross estate does not exceed £70,000; *and*
- The estate does not include DMCs or trust property; *and*
- The estate does not include foreign property exceeding in value £10,000; *and*
- The deceased had made no lifetime transfers within seven years of death; *and*
- The deceased had a UK domicile at death.

(If the PRs subsequently discover further assets which cause the estate to cease to be exempt, an account must be delivered within six months of the discovery.)

ii) The forms

Form 200 or form 202 must be completed and signed by the PRs as appropriate.

Form 202 is used where:

- the total net estate (after the deduction of exemptions, debts and reliefs) does not exceed £118,000; *and*
- the estate does not include DMCs or trust property; *and*
- all the property is situate in the UK; *and*
- the deceased made no lifetime transfers within seven years of death; *and*
- the deceased had a UK domicile at death; *and*
- the deceased did not, within seven years of death, have any interest in settled property or settle any property himself.

Form 200 is used in all other cases provided the deceased died domiciled in the UK.

iii) Payment of IHT

IHT on the deceased's free estate (see chapter 9) and on any settled land which devolves on the PRs (but excepting IHT on property where a right to pay by instalments exists) is payable on the delivery of the account, and must be paid before the grant will be issued.

IHT becomes due six months after the end of the month of death. Unpaid IHT becomes liable to interest from the date IHT is due.

Methods of raising money to pay the IHT.

- Assets which can be realised without the production of the grant: orders under the Administration of Estates (Small Payments) Act 1965; life policies held in trust for a third party; nominations; DMCs.
- Insurance companies and building societies may pay money directly to the Revenue on account of IHT without the production of the grant.
- Loans from beneficiaries.
- Loans from a bank. If this is done, the PRs should give the solicitor their irrevocable authority to give an undertaking to the bank that the loan will be repaid from the proceeds of the estate. Income tax relief is available for one year on interest paid on such a loan in so far as the IHT relates to personalty which vests in the PRs.
- Funeral payment or other Social Security entitlement.

f) *Proceedings in the Probate Registry*

i) Caveats

A caveat can be entered by any person who opposes the issue of a grant, to prevent the sealing of the grant in favour of any person without notice to the caveator. Written notice is given to and lodged at the Registry. It lasts for six months and can then be renewed if necessary.

No grant will be issued whilst the caveat is effective.

ii) Citations

Intended PRs should serve a citation on any caveator or on any person with a better title to the grant. The caveator or other can then:

- withdraw the caveat, if relevant or do nothing for eight days after which time any caveat becomes ineffective; *or*
- enter an appearance at the Registry or issue and serve summons for directions at the Registry.

If no appearance is entered for eight days or if a grant is not taken out within a reasonable time, the intended PRs can apply for the grant.

A citation can also be used by any person interested in the estate, to call upon an executor who has intermeddled with the estate to take out a grant.

If the executor does not make an appearance within eight days, the interested person can either:

- obtain an order requiring the executor to take out a grant; *or*
- take out the grant themselves.

iii) Standing search facility

This is an alternative to a caveat if the applicant simply wants to be informed of any issue of grant.

An application form and fee is lodged at the Registry. If a grant has been issued within 12 months before or is issued within six months after the application, an office copy is sent to the applicant. Extensions are possible.

g) *After the issue of the grant*

i) Death of a proving PR

If there are other PRs, they will continue with all the powers of the original PRs.

If the deceased PR is the sole or last surviving executor, his executor will become the executor of the testator provided that the 'chain of representation' has not been broken.

The chain of representation will be broken if:

- the executor predeceases the testator; *or*
- the executor fails to prove the will; *or*
- the executor dies intestate; *or*
- the executor fails to appoint his own executor.

If the chain is broken, a 'grant de bonis non administratis' will be required where part of the deceased's estate remains unadministered on the death of the sole or last surviving PR and a prior grant of representation has been made.

ii) Amendment and revocation of the grant

If the registrar is satisfied that a grant should be amended or revoked, he can make an order to this effect. Any amendment will not affect transactions between the PRs and third parties bona fide and for valuable consideration. Beneficiaries who have wrongly received assets are liable to return them or refund the correct beneficiary.

6 ASCERTAINING THE BENEFICIAL ENTITLEMENT

6.1 Introduction

It is the duty of the PRs to identify the beneficiaries who are entitled to a share in the estate, to ascertain the nature and the extent of their beneficial interest and then to distribute the estate accordingly. If the PRs distribute incorrectly, they will owe a personal responsibility to those whose rights they knew or should have known about.

6.2 Key points

a) *Construction of the will*

If any problems arise when construing the will, a construction summons should be taken out to protect PRs.

Rules of construction:

i) The court construes the will to give effect to the testator's intention as disclosed by the will as a whole, giving particular expressions and descriptions their *natural meaning* unless the contrary appears from the context.

ii) The court may take account of extrinsic evidence including evidence of the testator's intention where any part of the will is meaningless or where it contains a patent or latent ambiguity (eg if the description fits more than one person or thing).

iii) Where the court is satisfied that the will fails to carry out the testator's intentions because of a clerical error or of a failure to understand his instructions, it may order that the will be rectified so as to carry out those intentions. It will not do so if the draughtsman understood the instructions but simply mistook the legal effect of the words selected.

An application for a construction order must be made within six months of the date of the grant.

b) *Beneficiaries*

i) Statutory presumptions:

- No distinction is made between legitimate and illegitimate children.
- Adopted children are presumed to be children of the adoptive, and not the natural, parents.

- A legitimated person can take any interest as if he were born legitimate.

All of the above are subject to contrary intention shown in the will.

ii) Class-closing rules

If there is a gift to a class but no indication of when membership is to be determined, the following rules apply:

- Immediate vested gift - if at the testator's death, a member of the class exists, then the class closes then. If there is not, the class remains open indefinitely.
- Postponed vested gift - the class closes when the postponement ends. However, if no member has attained a vested interest until then, the class remains open indefinitely.
- Immediate contingent gift - the class closes at the testator's death if there is then in existence a member of the class who has satisfied the contingency. If there is not, the class closes when one member satisfies the contingency.
- Postponed contingent gift - the class closes when the postponement ends if there was living after the testator's death a member who has satisfied the contingency. If there was not, the class closes when one member satisfies the contingency.

In the cases of immediate and postponed contingent gifts (above), all members take, when the class closes, subject to fulfilling the contingency. If a member dies without doing so, his share is distributed between those who do.

- A gift of a fixed amount to each member of the class - the class closes at the testator's death, subject to any contrary intention being shown in the will.

iii) Identity of beneficiaries

The will speaks from the date of execution, subject to contrary intention, or from the date of any subsequent codicil. PRs must see who fitted the description at the date of will. If no one did, the gift will go to the first person who fits the description.

Before distributing, the PRs must satisfy themselves as to the identity of the beneficiaries by:

- facts within their personal knowledge; *and/or*
- certificates of birth, marriage or death; *and/or*
- statutory declarations as to pedigree by responsible persons.

If a beneficiary is known to have existed but can not be traced, the PRs should:

- firstly, advertise for information in a newspaper circulating in the locality where the person was last heard of; *then*
- if the beneficiary does not come forward, consider an application to court for a 'Benjamin order' or obtain indemnity from the other beneficiaries and/or obtain insurance cover.

In any event, the PRs should advertise under the Trustee Act 1925 s27 (see chapter 7).

iv) Lapse

A gift will lapse if the beneficiary predeceases the testator. There will be no lapse if:

- the will includes an effective substitute gift; *or*
- the gift is to joint tenants or is a class gift; *or*
- the gift is to discharge a moral obligation existing at the testator's death; *or*
- the gift is to a charitable institution which has ceased to exist or is for charitable purposes which cannot be carried out, but the will discloses a general charitable intention; *or*
- the gift is saved by Wills Act 1837 s33. This provides that if a gift is to the testator's child or remoter descendant who predeceases the testator but leaves issue living or en ventre sa mére at the testator's death, the gift does not lapse, but takes effect as a gift to such issue (per stirpes) subject to contrary intention being shown by the will.

v) Commorientes

Law of Property Act 1925 s184 - if two or more persons die in circumstances where it is impossible to determine the order of death, then for the purposes of succession to property the elder is deemed to die first.

This rule can be excluded by use of a survivorship clause. It does not apply for IHT purposes (the persons will be treated as dying at the same instant). Nor does it apply as between a husband and wife if the elder dies wholly or partially intestate; the younger will be treated as dying first for the purpose of property passing under the intestacy of the elder.

vi) Interests

Vested - a gift is vested if it depends only on the beneficiary being alive at the testator's death. If the beneficiary dies before obtaining possession of the gift, the benefit of the gift will devolve as part of the beneficiary's estate.

Contingent - a gift is contingent if it can only take effect when some future condition is satisfied. If the beneficiary dies before this, no benefit accrues to his estate.

c) *Property*

i) Construction

Wills Act 1837 s24 - the will speaks from the date of death, subject to contrary intention. Contrary intention will be shown by:

- the use of the word 'my' plus a gift of specific item owned by the deceased at the date of will. (If however, the gift of property is capable of increase or decrease - eg all my shares - this will not constitute contrary intention.)
- the use of the words 'now' and 'at present' if they are an essential part of the description.

ii) Ademption

If the testator's estate at death does not include anything which answers the description of a specific gift, the gift is adeemed and the beneficiary takes nothing, unless the subject matter of the gift was disposed of during the testator's lifetime and replaced by an asset answering the same description.

iii) Abatement

If the estate does not contain sufficient assets to achieve the provisions of the will, legacies will 'abate' (reduce proportionately). The order of priority is (from the top):

- specific and demonstrative legacies;
- general legacies;
- residue.

If the estate is insufficient to satisfy the legacies in a particular class, the legacies will abate proportionately inter se.

7 ADMINISTRATION OF THE ESTATE

7.1 Introduction

The administration of the deceased's estate fall to the PRs, on whom the deceased's assets generally devolve. The PRs must, therefore, be safeguarded against personal liability to creditors and other persons with claims against the estate.

7.2 Key points

a) *The PRs*

i) Duties

The PRs are under a duty to get in the estate of the deceased and to administer it according to the law 'with reasonable diligence'. The duty involves the collection and realisation of the assets; the payment of debts and legacies; and the distribution of the residue among those who are beneficially entitled.

ii) Powers

The PRs have powers conferred by the will, in addition to those conferred by statute (see chapter 2).

The powers are fiduciary in nature. The PRs must act bona fide and not profit unless authorised to do so.

iii) Safeguards

Administrative action - the court can make an order for the administration of the estate by the court. An application can be made by the PRs or by any other person interested in the estate.

Guidance by the court - the PRs or any other interested party can apply to the court to determine any question or to grant specific relief, as appropriate.

Statutory advertisement - Trustee Act 1925 s27 - PRs are protected against claims from creditors or beneficiaries of whom they have no notice if they:

- advertise for creditors and claimants by notice in:

  London Gazette; *and*

  local newspapers circulating in the district where any land owned by the deceased was situated; *and* any other appropriate publications in which the court would have ordered notices in an administrative action; *and*

- distributes after the time stated in the notice; *and*
- (in the case of land) makes the same searches as as independent purchasers of land would make.

Inheritance (Provision for Family and Dependants) Act 1975 (see chapter 3).

PRs should wait six months before distributing the estate in order to wait for any claims under this Act.

b) *Winding-up the solvent estate*

i) Collection and realisation of assets

Loans to pay IHT - these are repayable from the first assets realised.

Evidence to title - the original grant (endorsed with a memorandum of sale) is necessary to show title to land. In all other cases, an office copy will be sufficient.

Choice of assets to use for administration purposes - the PRs can use any assets but their choice will be influenced by:

- the ultimate incidence of liabilities in the estate;
- the possibility of substantial changes in the value of particular assets;
- the wishes of the beneficiaries;
- tax considerations (see chapter 9).

ii) Payment of debts

PRs are under a duty to pay the debts of the deceased with due diligence. If they fail to do so, they will be personally liable for any loss.

No strict rule exists as to the time for payment. However, if debts are still outstanding one year after death, the onus is on the PRs to justify the delay.

The duty is owed to creditors and beneficiaries. The duty to the beneficiaries, but not to creditors, can be modified by the will.

The duty can be enforced by:

- an order in administrative proceedings;
- an order for an inventory and account of the administration of the estate;
- a suit against the PRs for breach of duty.

Unsecured creditors

In the absence of any direction in the will, the order of assets to be applied for the payment of debts is determined by the statutory order in Administration of Estates Act 1925 Schedule I, part II (starting with the first):

- property undisposed of by will (including a lapsed share of residue) subject to a retention of funds to meet any pecuniary legacies.

  'Residue' - gross assets less specific gifts.

  'Pecuniary legacy' - includes an annuity, general legacy, demonstrative legacy in so far as it is not discharged out of designated property and any general direction for the payment of money such as a gift free of IHT.
- property comprised in a residuary gift, subject to the retention of a fund to meet any pecuniary legacies in so far as not provided for under (i) above.
- property specifically given for the payment of debts.
- property specifically charged with the payment of debts.
- the pecuniary legacy fund set aside in (i) and (ii) above.
- property specifically devised or bequeathed (rateably according to its value to the testator).
- property appointed under a general power.
- property subject to an option given by the will; DMCs; nominated property.

The statutory order is subject to contrary intention. This is generally shown by:

- common form trust for sale of the residue directing payment out of the net proceeds of sale before division; or
- gifts of residue which are expressed to be 'subject to' or 'after payment of' debts; or
- gifts of specific property for the payment of debts where an additional intention is shown to exonerate the other property.

Secured creditors

Administration of Estates Act 1925 s35 - where the deceased's estate contains property which is charged with debts, the property bears that charge subject to contrary intention.

Charges include:

- mortgages;
- vendor's lien for unpaid purchase money;
- lien in favour of a limited company over its own shares;
- charging orders.

Contrary intention is generally shown by:

- common form trust for sale of the residue directing the payment of the charge out of the proceeds of sale;

- a gift in the will expressly stated to be free from the charge;
- a general direction to pay the debts from a specific fund other than the residue.

NB: If the deceased has a mortgage protection policy payable to his estate it will not automatically be used to discharge the mortgage. It may, therefore be advisable to assign the benefit of the policy to the person who is to take the property.

Marshalling

A creditor can enforce a debt against any assets of the estate regardless of the terms of the will or of the statutory order.

If the assets *are* applied out of order, any beneficiary who is deprived of his benefit as a result can marshal other assets to compensate himself out of property which should have been used to pay debts in priority to his property.

Taxes and supplementary benefits

The Inland Revenue as a creditor of the deceased will be paid in the same order as the other creditors, but the PRs should also:

- make final returns (of income tax, CGT and IHT) to the date of the deceased's death. The liability is the deceased's, not the PRs'. The deceased is entitled to a full year's income tax relief in the year of death; *and*
- discharge any outstanding liabilities or reclaim any refunds due.

iii) Payment of general legacies (pecuniary legacies as previously defined).

The will may direct which assets are to be used. If it does not, the order of priority is as follows (subject to contrary intention):

- undisposed of property including a lapsed share of the residue; *then*
- general residuary personalty (with abatement if necessary). If the residue is not divided into realty and personalty, residuary realty can be used if residuary personalty proves insufficient.

Payment should be made with due diligence and generally within one year.

Interest on legacies is payable from the time payment falls due:

- the time fixed in the will; *or, if none,*
- one year after the date of death if the gift is vested when the contingency is attained if the gift is contingent.

Interest will be carried from death if:

- the legacy is in satisfaction of a debt; *or*

- the legacy is charged on unconverted realty (ie not on express trust for sale); *or*
- the legacy is to the testator's infant child or a child to whom the testator stands in loco parentis (subject to certain conditions); *or*
- the legacy is to any child to provide maintenance for him.

iv) Distribution of the residuary estate

Procedure:

- Adjust IHT assessment to take into account any changes in the assets or liabilities by submitting a corrective account to the Revenue.

  If an account was *not required*, an automatic discharge will be given to the PRs within 35 days of the grant.

  If an account was *submitted*, send the Revenue a Cap form 30 for a certificate of discharge from any further claims for IHT.
- Make a return of income and capital gains for the administration period (see chapter 9).
- Prepare estate accounts of the administration period. (Income and Capital accounts are generally separated.)
- Estate accounts should be approved and signed by the PRs and by the residuary legatee. This releases the PRs from further responsibility.
- Distribute to those entitled:

  Land - vest legal estate by assent in writing (and under seal if the assentee enters into covenants with the PRs). The assent must name the person in whose favour it is given and should contain an acknowledgment of the right to the production of the grant. A memorandum of assent should be endorsed on the original grant.

  shares - vest legal title by a share transfer form.

  chattels - pass title by delivery.

  bank/building society accounts - transfer forms exist.

  premium bonds - can not be transferred. They can be left until 12 months after the date of death and then cashed.

c) *Winding-up the insolvent estate*

An estate is insolvent if the assets are insufficient to pay all funeral, testamentary and administrative expenses, debts and liabilities.

Insolvency Act 1986 - order of discharge:

i) funeral, testamentary and administrative expenses;

ii) preferential debts (including secured creditors);

iii) ordinary debts;

iv) deferred debts.

Debts within each category rank pari passu. If insufficient assets exist to discharge the whole of a category, the debts will abate proportionately.

8 QUESTIONS (POST-DEATH)

QUESTION 1

Document Provided: Oath for Executor

You are consulted by Adam Post and Bernard Stanley in their capacity as executors of the late Cuthbert Dane. You are also consulted by Cuthbert's only daughter, Olive Evans, who is a widow.

Cuthbert lived at 33 Weyford Crescent, Weyford, Surrey. He died a widower aged 85 on 1st July 1986, domiciled in England and Wales.

Cuthbert's will gives his whole estate to Olive. The will makes no other dispositions. Olive, a millionairess aged 60, is very ill and likely to die soon. She tried, but failed to persuade Cuthbert to make a new will giving his estate to her issue, instead of to her.

Cuthbert's estate is valued at £160,000 gross. There are debts of £30,000.

Olive asks whether Cuthbert's estate can still be given to her issue direct. She wishes to avoid any personal liability to tax as a result of any such arrangement. Olive had three children: Philip and Rose who are adults and Gordon, who died in 1984. Gordon left three children, one of whom, Shayne, was born after Gordon's death. All three are still living and are minors.

Olive wants Philip, Rose and the issue of Gordon to benefit in equal shares, Gordon's issue taking his share equally between them. She insists that all their entitlements are to be vested. She considers this will simplify matters and cut administrative expenses.

(a) From a succession point of view only, explain:

(i) Whether or not complete effect can be given to Olive's wish by means of her simply disclaiming her entitlement under Cuthbert's will.

5 marks

(ii) Whether, if a disclaimer will not be fully satisfactory, an alternative is available to Olive to achieve her object.

3 marks

(b) (i) How, if at all, could the distribution of Cuthbert's estate direct to Olive's issue be achieved without involving Olive in a personal liability either to IHT or CGT?

(ii) In the context of your answer advise in the case of each tax whether there are any time limits or other statutory requirements and, if so, what.

(iii) State the consequences, if any, with regard to both IHT and CGT of Olive failing to take action within these time limits.

16 marks

(c) Assume that Olive's Will leaves her whole estate to Philip (one-third) and Gordon's children (one-third); (ie so that Olive's beneficiaries and their interests are identical to those whom she wishes to take Cuthbert's estate).

Advise her, purely from an IHT standpoint, whether there is any advantage to be gained by her re-directing Cuthbert's estate in her lifetime, since, if they survive her, those who benefit under her will in effect become entitled to Cuthbert's estate in any event on Olive's death.

8 marks

No calculations are necessary, but you should explain the main principles involved in your answer.

(d) Complete the form of Oath supplied on the following assumptions and taking into account also the facts provided above except as varied below:

(i) Olive's health improves and she decides to benefit under Cuthbert's will as drawn;

(ii) Adam Post dies before Cuthbert;

(iii) Bernard Stanley renounces probate;

(iv) Olive obtains the Grant at the Brighton District Registry;

(v) Olive instructs your firm Bligh Green & Co, of 13 Thames Parade, Weyford, Surrey, to act on her behalf (your reference is OM/5);

(vi) Olive wishes to affirm. Her address is 10 Princes Row, Haxford, Surrey; she had no occupation.

(vii) No settled land is involved.

10 marks

42 marks

Law Society Solicitors' Final Examination
Wills, Probate and Administration Summer 1986 Q2

QUESTION 1 - SOLUTION

General comment

This question could have been perfectly satisfactorily answered by mastery of four pages of the core material. It was rather repetitive in places and defective, on the facts given, in Question 1(a)(i). By and large a most disappointing paper.

Suggested solution

a) i) Where a beneficiary disclaims a gift in a will the property will pass as if that beneficiary had predeceased the testator. The destination of the disclaimed property thereafter depends on the nature of the gift: if the gift is residuary the property passes as under the intestacy rules. In this instance there is no gift over in the event of Olive failing to take so, if she disclaimed, Cuthbert's estate would pass under the intestacy rules. In accordance with s46 Administration of Estates Act 1925, Olive herself would take because she would rank as 'issue' of Cuthbert, being a daughter.

This would necessitate a further disclaimer by Olive of her beneficial interest under the intestacy, in which event Olive's issue would inherit, subject to the statutory trusts of the Administration of Estates Act: a disclaimer under an intestacy is allowed - see *Re Scott* (1975). Assuming, therefore, that Olive would disclaim her intestacy entitlement the estate of Cuthbert would devolve upon Philip and Rose, as to one-third share each. Gordon, the other child of Cuthbert, has left three children, one of them posthumously. Since all three are minors any entitlement they may have on a stirpital basis would be contingent until the statutory trusts are fulfilled. Philip and Rose would therefore have the prospect of sharing in this remaining one-third should the contingency not be satisfied. Clearly, Olive's wishes cannot be effected, because:

- not all the entitlements will be vested; and
- disclaimer under the will does not automatically bring about disclaimer under the intestacy which, as outlined, requires further action.

ii) There is an alternative for Olive to consider. She could enter into a variation of Cuthbert's estate. The beneficiaries here will not need to be parties nor will the executors, as the variation would lead to no increase in the IHT payable by reason of Cuthbert's death, although it is a customary process to join the executors in the variation. The variation will therefore provide a solution where someone has inherited property, as here, which he or she does not wish to pass to the person next entitled under the deceased's will or the intestacy rules.

b) i) A disclaimer would not require any further action by Olive and there would be no liability upon Olive for either tax, but a disclaimer, for reasons already given, would not achieve Olive's objective. A variation would result in a personal liability upon Olive to CGT and IHT (where she would be taxed as transferor). This prima facie liability can, however, be avoided by Olive making a written election that the terms of the variation will be treated as having been incorporated into Cuthbert's will. Similarly, in order to avoid CGT Olive must make an election.

The two elections may be made in one document or may be made separately. The document must refer to the respective statutory provisions enabling the power to take place.

ii) In order for Olive's variation to be treated as part of Cuthbert's will both for IHT and CGT purposes it must comply with certain requirements concerning time-limits:

- the variation must be made within two years of Cuthbert's death;

- the election must be made within six months of the variation: the Revenue does have a discretion in this regard but it would be unwise to rely upon their exercising it in favour of Olive.

Both the documents of variation and election are required to be produced to the Capital Taxes Office and to the Inspector of Taxes.

iii) The variation would still be effective. The tax consequences for Olive would be that she would be treated as having made a lifetime chargeable transfer to her issue at the date of the variation. Accordingly, she would be liable to IHT in respect of that transfer at the lifetime rates and Cuthbert's executors would still be liable at the death rates for the transfer upon death. For the purposes of CGT Olive would be treated as making a disposal of the assets at the date of the variation: if at that time their value exceeded their value at Cuthbert's death, after indexation, she would be liable to pay CGT on the gain, subject to the availability of her personal CGT exemption, any unutilised losses and an election being made for the gain to be 'held over'.

c) Cuthbert's estate has a net value of £130,000. Assuming that Cuthbert made no chargeable lifetime transfers, £128,000 of the estate is within the nil rate band for IHT and the total IHT bill will only be a small proportion of the estate (about £800, ie negligible).

After receiving Cuthbert's estate Olive's estate would be approximately £1 million plus £130,000 ie £1,130,000. Upon Olive's death her estate would attract IHT at 40 per cent. This would mean, ignoring any quick succession relief or growth in value, that her issue would ultimately receive from Cuthbert only 60 per cent of £130,000. Any quick succession relief would be modest in any event, given that very little IHT payable on Cuthbert's estate.

The advice to Adam, Bernard and Olive should therefore be that the variation is worthwhile since, by keeping Cuthbert's assets out of Olive's estate, there is a lower overall bill for IHT and hence the issue of Olive will benefit more than if the assets of Cuthbert suffer IHT both on Olive's death as well as on his death before finally reaching them.

d) Completed Oath for Executors (see pages 86-87).

Oath for Executors

IN THE HIGH COURT OF JUSTICE

Extracting Solicitor Bligh, Green & Co (Ref OM/5)

Address 13, Thames Parade, Weyford, Surrey

Family Division

THE ~~PRINCIPAL REGISTRY~~ District Probate Registry at Brighton

IN the Estate of* Cuthbert Dane deceased.

(1) I, Olive Evans, of 10 Princes Row, Haxford, Surrey, widow

~~make Oath and say, (2)~~ do solemnly and sincerely affirm that

(1) believe the paper writing now produced to and marked by (3) me

to contain the true and original last Will and Testament (4)

of* Cuthbert Dane

of 33, Weyford Crescent, Weyford, Surrey

~~formerly of~~

deceased

who died on the 1st day of July 1986,

aged 85 years (5) domiciled in (6) England and Wales

and that to the best of my knowledge, information and belief there was (7) [no] land vested in the said deceased which was settled previously to his death (and not by his Will (4))

and which remained settled land notwithstanding his death (8)

~~And I/we further make oath and say (2) that notice of this application has been given to~~

~~the executor(s) to whom power is to be reserved, [save~~

*If necessary to include alias of deceased in grant add "otherwise (alias name)" and state below which is true name and reason for requiring alias.

(1) "I" *or* "We". Insert the full name, place of residence and occupation or, if none, description of the deponent(s), adding "Mrs", "Miss", as appropriate, for a female deponent.

(2) *Or* "do solemnly and sincerely affirm".

(3) Each testamentary paper must be marked by each deponent, and by the person administering the oath.

(4) "with one, two (or more) Codicils", as the case may be.

(5) If exact age is unknown, give best estimate.

(6) Where there are separate legal divisions in one country, the state, province, etc., should be specified.

(7) Delete "no", if there was land vested in deceased which remained settled land notwithstanding his death.

(8) Settled land may be included in the scope of the grant provided the executors are also the special executors as to the settled land; in that case the settlement must be identified.

(9) Delete or amend as appropriate. Notice of this application must be served on all executors to whom power is to be reserved unless dispensed with by a registrar under Rule 27 (3).

(10) "I am" *or* "we are". Insert relationship of the executors to the deceased only if necessary to establish title or identification.

(11) "The sole", *or* "the surviving", *or* "one of the", *or* "are the", *or* "two of the", etc.

(12) If there was settled land and the grant is to include it, insert "including settled land" but, if the grant is to exclude the settled land, insert "save and except settled land".

(13) Complete this paragraph only if the deceased died on or after 1 April 1981 and an Inland Revenue Account is not required; the next paragraph should be deleted.

(14) Insert "100,000" in respect of deaths on or after 1 April 1989, "70,000 in respect of deaths on or after 1 April 1987, "40,000" in respect of deaths on or after 1 April 1983 or "25,000" in respect of deaths prior to that date.

(15) Insert currently "10,000", "25,000", "40,000", "70,000", or "100,000" as appropriate.

(16) Complete this paragraph only if an Inland Revenue Account is required and delete the previous paragraph.

N.B. The names of all executors to whom power is to be reserved must be included in the Oath.

And I further do solemnly and sincerely affirm that]. [9]
Adam Post one of the executors named in the said will
~~And (1)~~ ~~further make Oath and say (2)~~ predeceased the deceased and
~~that (10) (11)~~ Bernard Stanley, the
other executor named in the said will has renounced ~~Execut~~
~~named in the said~~ probate thereof and that I am the residuary
beneficiary named in the said will of the said deceased
and that (1) I will (i) collect, get in and administer according to the law the real and personal estate (12) of the said deceased; (ii) when required to do so by the Court, exhibit on oath in the Court a full inventory of the said estate (12)
and when so required render an account of the administration of the said estate to the Court; and (iii) when required to do so by the High Court, deliver up the grant of probate to that Court; and that to the best of my knowledge, information and belief

~~(13) [the gross estate passing under the grant does not exceed (14) £ and the net estate does not exceed (15) £ , and that this is not a case in which an Inland Revenue Account is required to be delivered]~~

(16) [the gross estate passing under the grant amounts to £ 160,000 and the net estate amounts to £ 130,000].

*

SWORN by Deponent Olive Evans the above-named

at

this day of 19 ,

Before me,

(independent solicitor)
A Commissioner for Oaths/Solicitor.

QUESTION 2

Document Provided: IHT 200

As a partner in A, B & C, solicitors of Northtown, Nottinghamshire, you receive instructions from Joan Jones of 1 Church Street, Northtown and her brother George Green of 12 Church Street, Northtown to prove the Will of Joan's late husband, Fred. At the time of his death Fred lived with Joan. He was born on 16 August 1921 and died on 11 December, 1986. He was employed as an accountant by X, Y and Z.

As well as being survived by Joan, Fred left two children. Both his parents died before him.

By his will Fred left the whole of his estate to Joan and appointed her and George Green as executors.

Jointly with Joan, Fred had a share account in the Northtown Building Society which at death contained £6,000, plus accrued interest of £300,00.

The assets which he held in his own name at death were as follows (figures given as at death):

Freehold house: 1 Church Street, Northtown as valued by Smith & Smith, Chartered Surveyors	£80,000.00
Personal effects (estimated)	2,600.00
Westbank, Northtown deposit account	3,500.00
Westbank, Northtown deposit account interest	200.00
Westbank, Northtown current account	1,200.00
Renault car (this has already been sold by the executors for the figure shown)	2,400.00
Salary due to the date of death	600.00
Cash	300.00
National Savings Certificate	4,500.00

The liabilities of the estate are:

Loan from Northdown Building Society on the security of 1 Church Street	3,000.00
Northtown Funeral Services Limited (including £200.00 for tombstone)	600.00
East Midland Electricity Board	80.00
Northtown District Council - rates	250.00
Income Tax due to death (estimated)	600.00

Under Fred's employer's pension scheme there is a lump sum of £5000.00 payable on his death. It is payable at the discretion of the trustees of the scheme, but it transpires that Fred, during his life, asked the trustees that the amount concerned should be paid to his widow.

Fred also paid premiums on an insurance policy on his own life. This was for £10,000.00 and was with the Equity Insurance Company Limited. It was written in trust for the absolute benefit of Joan.

Fred did not within the ten years before his death make any lifetime transfers which were either chargeable to inheritance tax or which used up any part of the 'nil rate band' for the purpose of that tax.

Finally, Fred was the tenant for life under the will of his late father Bernard Jones. The accountants to the trust have prepared a statement at death as follows:

Bernard Jones's will trust:	
Investments (as valued)	£ 28,900.00
Cash capital (uninvested)	150.00
Income accrued to death of Fred Jones	50.00

Note:

(i) Following the death of the tenant for life the whole fund passes to charity.

(ii) The trustees are the Westbank Trust Company Limited.

(iii) The Capital Taxes Office reference is 333.

(a) Explain the inheritance tax position. In your answer you should deal with Fred's estate (including the Building Society share account), the Bernard Jones's will trust and the insurance and pension benefits. **7 marks**

(b) Complete the Inland Revenue Account (IHT form 200 supplied) as far as you can from the information given. You should confine your answer solely to the insertion in the form supplied of such of the above information as you consider relevant.

Please do not complete page 11 of the form. **17 marks**

(c) In what ways may Joan be able to obtain cash without waiting for the grant to come through? **9 marks**

33 marks

Adapted from Law Society Solicitors' Final Examination
Wills, Probate and Administration Winter 1987 Q2

QUESTION 2 - SOLUTION

General comment

This consisted of three sub-questions comprising a total of 33 marks. Part (b) required a candidate, for 17 marks, to complete an Inland Revenue Account (IHT 200) and was the best example of its kind yet devised by the examiner; part (a) was equally convincing but surely merited more than the seven marks allotted considering the amount of detail required, whereas part (c) was straightforward and of limited detail: it is somewhat surprising, therefore, that it carried nine marks and many students must have been wondering if they had omitted essential content from their answers.

Suggested solution

a) The assets of which Fred was competent to dispose at the date of his death, both in relation to non-instalment option property, and instalment option property, are prima facie liable to inheritance tax as chargeable transfers; however, Fred left all his estate to his surviving spouse, Joan. Accordingly, all the transfers of value will be exempt under the spouse exemption provisions in so far as the value transferred becomes comprised in the estate of Joan.

   The building society share account in Northtown Building Society was held by Fred and Joan jointly as beneficial joint-tenants. Joan becomes absolutely entitled to the fund by survivorship and it will not devolve on the deceased's personal representatives. A joint-tenancy cannot be severed by will.

   The effect of Fred's death is of significance to the Bernard Jones's will trust. The fund now passes to charity and the settlement comes to an end. Fred has enjoyed an interest in possession as life-tenant. He is treated for tax purposes as having owned the trust property, and the termination by death of his interest in possession constitutes a taxable disposition of the entire value of the trust property. The rate of tax is in principle dependant upon that person's cumulative total - here nil - and upon whether the termination is on death - as here - or during lifetime. It should be noted that the charity cannot claim exemption from tax because, as with spouse exemption, the gift must be immediate (which here it is not).

   As regards the insurance policy on Fred Jones's life in the sum of £10,000 with Equity Insurance Company Ltd for the benefit of his wife, Joan, it would appear that the policy has been written under s11 Married Women's Property Act 1882. Under this provision a policy of life insurance effected by a person on his own life can, as here, be expressed to be for the benefit of his spouse and/or children. This creates a trust in their favour and on Fred's death, in the facts of the problem, the sum insured will be paid direct to the trustees of the policy for the benefit of the named beneficiary, Joan. There will be no inheritance tax charge arising in respect of the accused's estate (Fred) since the assured has no beneficial interest. Unless policies are written in the prescribed manner the insurance company pays the insured amount to the deceased's personal representatives and the sum paid will form part of his estate.

The lump sum of £5,000 under Fred's employer's pension scheme is one which permits a third party to benefit at the discretion of the trustees. In effect it is a 'discretionary pension scheme'. Usually, such a lump sum is only paid when the contributor dies 'in service'. Benefits of this type do not form part of the deceased's estate for inheritance tax purposes, and are thus treated like other discretionary trust distributions.

b) Completed Inland Revenue Account: IHT form 200 (see pages 92-115).

c) Provision is made under the Administration of Estates (Small Payments) Act 1965 for small sums to be paid or transferred on death without the need to produce a grant of representation. This power is discretionary. The upper limit on these payments is £5,000. The payment can be made in respect of money held in National Savings Bank, Savings Certificates, Premium Bonds, Trustee Savings Bank; also in respect of money invested in a building society. Accordingly, it would be possible on the facts for Joan to obtain the £4,500 of National Savings Certificates and £500 from the building society account without having to wait for grant of probate.

Realisation of assets without production of grant, apart from the 1965 statutory provision, can be achieved from life policies written under Married Women's Property Act 1882 (relevant here); nominations, and property formerly held jointly with the deceased (again, relevant here).

If Joan is herself in need of immediate financial provision she can have recourse to death grant and social security entitlement, or bank loan facilities - which may be required for payment of inheritance tax in anticipation of obtain grant. Joan and her fellow executor should obtain a grant of probate at an early date on these facts - within six weeks at the outside.

Inland Revenue
Inheritance Tax*

Inland Revenue Account

- For use where the deceased died on or after 18 March 1986 domiciled in the United Kingdom
- Please see IHT 210 for instructions on how to complete this form

* *Capital Transfer Tax in the case of a death before 25 July 1986*

Your reference	Name and address of solicitors ø A B & C Northtown Nottinghamshire Postcode
Your telephone number	

ø All communications concerning Inheritance Tax will be sent to the Solicitors unless the executors or administrators request otherwise.

For Official Use	
Date of Grant	

In the High Court of Justice Family Division (Probate)

The PRINCIPAL **Registry**

In the estate of FREDERICK JONES

Please use CAPITAL letters

Surname	JONES	Date of birth	16 08 1921
Title and Forenames	MR FREDERICK	Date of death	11 12 1986

Marital Status *Please tick as appropriate*

Married [✓] Single [ ] Divorced [ ] Widowed [ ]

Surviving Relatives

Husband [ ] Wife [✓] Child(ren) [✓] Parent(s) [ ]

Domicile

England and Wales [✓] Scotland [ ] N.Ireland [ ]

Last usual address

1 CHURCH STREET
NORTHTOWN
NOTTINGHAMSHIRE

Postcode

Occupation	ACCOUNTANT

Please state the Tax District at which the tax affairs of the deceased were handled		Tax District Reference

Please give the names and permanent addresses of the executors or intending administrators:

JOAN JONES 1 CHURCH STREET NORTHTOWN NOTTINGHAMSHIRE Postcode	Postcode
GEORGE GREEN 12 CHURCH STREET NORTHTOWN NOTTINGHAMSHIRE Postcode	Postcode

IHT200

1

Declaration

1. I/We desire to obtain a grant of PROBATE of the aforenamed deceased.

2. To the best of my/our knowledge and belief all the statements and particulars furnished in this account and its accompanying schedules are true and complete.

Delete paragraph if inappropriate

3. I/We have made the fullest enquiries that are reasonably practicable in the circumstances but have not been able to ascertain the exact value of the property referred to in Exhibit to section . So far as the value can now be estimated, it is stated in section . I/We undertake, as soon as the value is ascertained, to deliver a further account, and to pay both any additional tax payable for which I/We may be liable, and any further tax payable, for which I/We may be liable on the other property mentioned in this account.

**Delete what is inappropriate*

4. So far as the tax on the property disclosed in sections 1B, 2B and 3 may be paid by instalments, I/We elect to pay/not to pay* by instalments as indicated in these sections.

Signed by the above-named (Joan Jones)

date

Signed by the above-named (George Green)

date

Signed by the above-named

Warning

An executor or intending administrator who fails to make the fullest enquiries that are reasonably practicable in the circumstances may be liable to penalties.

He or she may be liable to penalties or prosecution if he or she fails to disclose in Section 1A, 1B, 2A, 2B and 3

date

Signed by the above-named

date

(as appropriate) and in his or her answers to the questions on page 3 and at the foot of page 9 all the property to the best of his or her knowledge and belief in respect of which tax may be payable on the death of the deceased.

Transfers of value which need not be reported are

a. gifts or other transfers of value made to the deceased's spouse unless at the time of transfer the deceased was domiciled in the United Kingdom and the spouse was not

b. gifts of money not exceeding £3,000 in any one year, where the executors or intending administrators are satisfied that they are wholly exempt as normal gifts out of income

c. outright gifts to one individual which are clearly exempt as not exceeding £250 in any one year (to 5 April): (for gifts before 6 April 1980 the exemption is restricted to £100 in any one year)

d. other gifts of money, or of shares or securities quoted on the Stock Exchange, where these, together with any other gifts not within (b) or (c) above do not in total exceed the exemption for gifts of £3,000 in any one year (to 5 April)

2

- Any property mentioned on this page which is subject to Inheritance Tax, whether or nor tax is actually payable, **must** also be included in sections 1A, 1B, 2A, 2B, or 3 of this account as appropriate. If it is claimed that the property is not subject to Inheritance Tax, reasons should be given.
- Even if a full report has been made or any other information relevant to the answers to any of the questions below has been given to an Inland Revenue Office, affirmative answers must nonetheless be given to the appropriate questions. Please also identify the office and quote any relevant official reference.
- Where necessary schedules may be attached.

1. Gifts etc.

Did the deceased, within 7 years of his/her death	*Please tick yes or no* yes	no	For official use only
• make any gift, settlement or other transfer of value other than a transfer mentioned in the notes on page 2.		✓	
• make any disposition for the maintenance of a relative		✓	Married Womens' Property Act policy. Equity Insurance Co. Ltd. Beneficiary: Joan Jones Value at death: £10,000
• pay any premium on a policy of life assurance not included in Section 1 of this form?	✓		
Did the deceased at any time on or after 18 March 1986 dispose of any property by way of gift where either			
• possession and enjoyment of the property was not bona fide assumed by the donee, or			
• the property was not enjoyed to the entire exclusion of the donor and of any benefit to him/her by contract or otherwise?			

If the reply to any of the questions above is "yes", please give full particulars including dates, details of any property affected and the names and addresses of the other parties concerned, on a separate sheet of paper.

2. Settled property

	yes	no	For official use only
• Was the deceased, at the time of his/her death, entitled to a life interest, annuity or other interest in possession in settled property whether as beneficiary under the settlement or otherwise?	✓		See Section 3. Bernard Jones' Will Trust.
• Did the deceased cease to be entitled to any such interest in settled property within 7 years of his/her death?		✓	

If the reply to either question is "yes", please give full particulars of the title (including, in the case of a Will/intestacy, the name and date of death of the testator/intestate and date and place of grant). Where the interest was under a settlement and no previous report has been made, kindly forward a copy of the settlement.

3. Nominations

Did the deceased in his lifetime nominate any Savings Bank Account, Savings Certificates or other assets in favour of any person? ☐ ☑

If you have answered "yes", please give full particulars in section 2 on page 8.

4. Joint property

Was the deceased joint owner of any property of any description or did he/she hold any money on a joint account (apart from property or money of which he/she was merely a trustee)? ☑ ☐

If you have answered "yes" please give the following details on a separate sheet of paper

Joint owner with spouse of funds with Northtown Building Society. See Section 2A

- the date when the joint ownership began (or the date of opening the joint account)
- The name(s) of the other joint owner(s)
- By whom and from what source the joint property was provided and, if it or its purchase price was contributed by one or more of the joint owners, the extent ot the contribution made by each
- how the income (if any) was dealt with and enjoyed
- whether the deceased's interest passed under his/her will or intestacy or by survivorship.

3

Section 1

A schedule of all the property of the deceased within the United Kingdom to which the deceased was beneficially entitled and **in respect of which the grant is made,** excluding property over which the deceased had and exercised by will a general power of appointment. The appointed property should be included in Section 3. Property gifted by the deceased subject to a reservation retained by the deceased should also be included in Section 3 rather than here.

Section 1A Property without the Instalment Option

For official use only

	Gross value at date of death*
Stocks, shares, debentures and other securities as set out in CAP 40:	
• **Quoted** in the Stock Exchange daily official list except so far as included in Section 1B	
• **Others,** except so far as included in Section 1B	
National Savings Certificates and interest to the date of death	
Uncashed dividents and **interest received, dividends declared,** and **interest accrued due,** in respect of the above investments, to the date of death, as statement annexed	
Cash at the bank:	
• On current account and interest (if any) to the date of death at: Westbank, Northtown	1,200
• On deposit and interest to the date of death at: Westbank, Northtown, 3500 + 200 interest	3,700
Cash (other than cash at banks)	300

	£	
Money at a National or Trustee Savings Bank and **interest** to the date of death, as statement annexed National Savings Certificates	4,500	
Money out on Mortgage, and **interest** to the date of death, as statement annexed		
Money with a building society, co-operative or friendly society, and **interest** to the date of death, as statement annexed		
Money out on promissary notes, bonds and other securities, and **interest** to the date of death, as statement annexed		
Other debts due to the deceased and **interest** to the date of death, except book debts included in Section 1B, as statement annexed		
Unpaid purchase money of real and leasehold property contracted in the lifetime of the deceased to be sold, as statement annexed		
Rents of the deceased's own real and leasehold property to the date of death		
Apportionment of the rents of the deceased's real and leasehold property to the date of death		
Income accrued due, but not received before the death, arising from real and personal property, in which the deceased had a life or other limited interest, viz:- income accrued under Bernard Jones Will Trust	50	
Apportionment of Income from that source to the date of death		
Any other income, apportioned where necessary, to which the deceased was entitled at his death (eg pensions, annuities, director's fees, etc) as statement annexed Salary due to date of death	600	
Policies of insurance and bonuses (if any) thereon, on the life of the deceased, as statement annexed		
Saleable value of policies of insurance and bonuses (if any) not payable on the death of the deceased, as statement annexed		
To be carried forward	10,350	

* *All claims for exemptions or reliefs should be made in the Summary on page 10*

4

Section 1A **Continued**

For official use only

	Gross value at date of death*
Brought forward	10,350
Household and personal goods, including pictures, china, linen, clothes, books plate, jewels, motor cars, boats, etc.	
Sold, realised gross £ 2,400 [Renault motor car]	
Unsold, estimated £ 2,600 [miscellaneous personal effects]	5,000

The deceased's interest expectant upon death of

aged years, under the will/intestacy of

who died on the
or under a settlement dated the
and made between

(setting out the parties to the deed), in the property set out in the statement annexed, of which fund the present trustees are

Tick as appropriate

Was the interest at any time acquired for value whether by the deceased or a predecessor in title? Yes ☐ No ☐

Income tax payable

Other personal property not comprised under the preceding heads
Please give details

Gross property not subject to the instalment option to be carried to page 6 and to the Probate Summary on page 12 15,350

** All claims for exemptions or reliefs shoud be made in the Summary on page 10*

5

Section 1A **continued**

Schedule of liabilities and funeral expenses. Particulars of the funeral expenses of the deceased and the liabilities due and owing from him at the time of his death to persons resident within the United Kingdom or to persons resident out of the United Kingdom but contracted to be paid in the United Kingdom, or charged on property situated within the United Kingdom (other than liabilities deducted in Section 1B or section 2 under footnote (b) on page 8).

Name and address of creditor	Description of liability	Amount	For official use only
East Midlands Electricity Board	Electricity Board	80	
Northtown District Council	Rates	250	
Inland Revenue	Income tax (estimated) due to death	600	

Funeral expenses

Northtown Funeral Services Ltd.	400
Total to be carried to the Summary below and to the Probate Summary on page 12	1,330

Summary

Gross property (from page 5) not subject to the instalment option	15,350
Less total of liabilities and funeral expenses from above	1,330
Net property in the United Kingdom not subject to the instalment option to be carried to page 11 (Section 1A, net total before relief(s)	14,020

Section 4 on page 9 must be completed in respect of all liabilities listed in the above schedule.

6

Section 1B — Property with the Instalment Option

For official use only

Tick as appropriate

- Is the tax on this property to be paid on delivery of this account? Yes ☐ No ☑
- Is payment to be made in yearly instalments? Yes ☑ No ☐

	Value at date of death
Land etc. owned by the deceased in the United Kingdom (not being settled land) whether or not subject to a trust for sale as described on Cap 37 annexed. 1, Church Street, Northtown (as per valuation attached)	80,000
Business interests	
• Net value of deceased's interest in the business(es), as statement or balance sheet annexed.	
• Net value of deceased's interest as partner in the firm of ________ as statement or balance sheet annexed	
Stocks, shares, debentures and other securities, as set out on Cap 40.	
• Shares or securities etc within Section 228(1) (a) Inheritance Tax Act 1984 which gave the deceased control of the company immediately before his death *see Section 269 Inheritance Tax Act 1984.*	
• Other unquoted shares or securities etc. within Section 228(1) (b) or (c) or (d) Inheritance Tax Act 1984 (all other unquoted shares to be included in Section 1A).	

Value of property within the instalment option to be carried to the Probate Summary on Page 12.	80,000

Liabilities charged at the date of the deceased's death on the property included above other than those already taken into account above

Particulars of liability	**Property on which charged**	**Amount**
Mortgage Loan Northtown Building Society	1, Church Street, Northtown, Nottinghamshire	3,000
Total liabilities to be carried to the Probate Summary on page 12.		3,000

Value of property with the instalment option less liabilities to be carried to page 11 (Section 1B, net total before reliefs).	77,000

* *All claims for exemptions and reliefs should be made in the Summary on page 10.*

Section 4 on page 9 must be completed in respect of all liabilities listed above

7

Section 2

All other property on which the personal representatives are liable to pay the tax (or would be liable if any tax were payable) including:-

- all nominated property and property passing by survivorship
- all property situated outside the UK

Section 2A - Property without the Instalment Option

Particulars of the property, local situation and details of disposition if nominated or in joint names	**Value at date of death**
Share account at Northtown Building Society (address) held by deceased and wife Joan Jones as beneficial joint tenants (value of entirety : 6300)	3,150
Gross Value (half share of deceased)	3,150

For official use only

Liabilities⁺ in respect of the property above

Name and Address of Creditor	**Description of liability**	**Amount**
	Total liabilities	

Net value to be carried to page 11 (Section 2A, net total before reliefs)	

Section 2B - Property with the Instalment Option

Tick as appropriate

- Is the tax on this property to be paid on delivery of this account? ☐ Yes ☐ No
- Is payment to be made by yearly instalments? ☐ Yes ☐ No

Particulars of the property, local situation and details of disposition if nominated or in joint names	Value at date of death
Gross Value	

Liabilities⁺ In respect of the property above

Name and Address of Creditor	Description of Liability	Amount
	Total liabilities	

Net value to be carried to page 11 (Section 2B, net total before reliefs) ☐

* *All claims for exemptions or reliefs should be made in the Summary on page 10*

\+ *Liabilities*
(a) due from the deceased at the time of his death to persons resident outside the United Kingdom (other than liabilities contracted to be paid in the United Kingdom, or charged on property within the United Kingdom which have been deducted in Sections 1A and 1B) or
(b) (so far as not included in (a) charged upon incurred in connection with or otherwise affecting the property included in this Section

Section 4 on page 9 must be completed in respect of all liabilities listed above.

Section 3

Any other property in the UK and elsewhere in which the deceased had or is treated as having had a beneficial interest in possession immediately before his death including:-

- property over which the deceased had and exercised by will a general power of appointment.
- property outside the UK comprised in a settlement made by a UK domiciled person.
- property gifted by the deceased subject to a reservation retained by the deceased.

Part 1 Property on which tax is elected to be paid on delivery of this account should be listed below and headed "Part 1"

- Is the tax on any property with the Instalment Option to be paid by yearly instalments? *Tick as appropriate*

  ☐ Yes ☐ No

- Separate net totals for Part 1 (property without the instalment option) and Part 1 (property with the instalment option) should be carried to page 11 (Sections 1a (non-instalment option property) and 1b (instalment option property) net totals before reliefs).

Part 2 Property on which tax is not to be paid on delivery of this account should be listed below and headed "Part 2" and its net value carried to page 11 (Section 1c, net total before reliefs).

Separate consecutive numbering for part 1 and part 2	**Particulars of the property**	**Net value at date of death** *		For official use only
		Property without the instalment option £	**Property with the instalment option** £	
Part 2	Bernard Jones Will Trust Ref: 333 The deceased was life tenant of a settlement			

	under the will of his late father Bernard Jones who died on (information required). Present trustee: Westbank Trust Co. Ltd.			
	Investments	28,900		
	Cash capital	150		
		29,050		

* *All claims for exemptions or reliefs should be made in the Summary on page 10*

Section 4

Deductions of liabilities listed in this account

In the case of any liability for which a deduction has been taken in either section 1A, 1B, 2A, 2B or 3 of this account did the consideration for any such debt or incumbrance incurred or created on or after 18 March 1986 consist of property derived from the deceased or was the consideration given by any person who was at any time entitled to, or amongst whose resources there was at any time included any property derived from the deceased?

Tick as appropriate

Yes ☐ No ☐

If "Yes", please give full particulars, including the liabilities in question, the consideration given and the derivation of that consideration from the deceased.

Please attach schedules as necessary.

Summary of exemptions and reliefs against capital

- please see instruction booklet IHT 210 as to how this page should be completed
- Schedules should be attached as necessary

Property in respect of which exemption or relief is claimed. The description should not be more detailed than is necessary to identify the property	Nature of exemption or relief claimed	Net value of property £	Amounts exemption or relief claimed £	For official use only
Property included in Section 1A The whole	Spouse - s18 Inheritance Tax Act 1984	14,020	14,020	
Total of exemptions and reliefs Section 1A to be carried to page 11 (reliefs column)				
Property included in Section 1B				

Freehold property 1, Church Street, Northtown, Nottinghamshire.	Spouse – s18 Inheritance Tax Act 1984	77,000	77,000

Total of exemptions and reliefs Section 1B to be carried to page 11 (reliefs column) [ ]

Property included in other sections - state and show separately which section (sections 2A and B and 3 (Part 1) and 3 (Part 2)
A separate total of exemptions and reliefs for each of these sections should be carried to page 11 (reliefs column)

Section 2A	Spouse – s18 Inheritance Tax Act 1984	3,150	3,150

10

Assessment of Inheritance Tax

Summary for determining chargeable rates

Section of accounts	Net total £	Reliefs £	Value of property after reliefs £
1(a) Property without the instalment option			
1A			
2A			
3, Part 1			
Total 1(a)			
1(b) Property with the instalment option			
1B			
2B			
3, Part 1			
Total 1(b)			
1(c) Other property on which tax is not being paid on this account			
3, Part 2			
Total 1(c)			
Total 1 (a) to (c)			**A**

Calculation of tax

	£	p
Tax on **C** on first £ plus on balance of £ @ %		
Total		
Less tax on **B** at death rate on first £ plus on balance of £ @ %		
Total		
Less QSR (as attached schedule)		
Total tax chargeable on **A**	**D**	

Any capital figure multiplied by $\frac{D}{A}$ gives the proportion of tax assessable on that capital

Value on which tax is now being paid

	Value of property	
	non-instalment £	Instalment option £
Total value at 1(a)		

Cumulative total of chargeable trans‑ers made prior to the deceased's death	B	That part of 1(b) on which tax now to be paid	
Aggregate chargeable transfers (A + B)	C		

Amount payable on this account

Non instalment property	£	p
Total value at 1(a) £ × $\frac{D}{A}$ =		
Less reliefs against tax other than QSR		
Net tax		
**add* interest on net tax from 19 to 19 (years days at %)		
Total tax and interest on non-instalment property (carried to page 12)		
Additional tax and interest due under S7 IHTA 1984-as attached schedule (carried to page 12)		

Instalment option property	£	p
That part of 1(b) on which tax now to be paid £ × $\frac{D}{A}$ =		
Less reliefs against tax other than QSR		
Net tax		
**add* interest on net tax from 19 to 19 (years days at %)		
Instalments - tenths of net tax		
add interest on instalments now assessed from 19 (date last instalment due) to 19 (days at %)		
†*add* interest on whole of net tax on instalment property from 19 to 19 (years days at %)		
Total tax and interest on instalment option property (carried to page 12)		

Interest

* Tax becomes due 6 months after the end of the month in which the death occurred. Unpaid tax carries interest from and including the day after the due date, irrespective of the reason for the late payment.

† Only if the due date for the second or subsequent instalment has now passed and interest relief (see IHT 210) is not in point, add here interest on the whole of the net tax on the instalment option property up to the due date of the last instalment.

Interest on overpaid tax; please note that, where tax or interest is paid in excess of the amount found to be due, interest is allowed on the amount overpaid.

11

Probate Summary

Aggregate Gross Value which in law devolves on and vests in the personal representatives of the deceased, for and in respect of which the Grant is to be made

	£
Section 1A	15,350
Section 1B	80,000
Section 3*	

* *absolute power property only*

	£
Total to be carried to the probate papers	95,350
Deduct	
Section 1A, total of liabilities and funeral expenses	1,330
Section 1B, total of liabilities	3,000
Net value for probate purposes	91,020

For official use only

Total of Tax and Interest from page 11

	£
Total Tax and Interest - Non-Instalment Property	
Total Tax and Interest - Instalment Option Property	

	Additional Tax and Interest due under S7 Inheritance Tax Act 1984
	Total tax and interest payable now on this account
EDP	On the basis of this Account the tax (and interest) payable now is
	________________ 19____ Solicitor(s) for the applicant(s)

This receipt and stamp do not imply that the assessment is not subject to rectification: the account will be fully examined after the issue of the grant.

Prints of this form and of the instructions (IHT 210) can be obtained from the Capital Taxes Office, Inland Revenue, Rockley Road, London W14 0DF and on personal application only at the Stamps Office, Room G3, South West Wing, Bush House, Strand, WC2B 4QN the London Chief Post Office, King Edward Street, EC1A 1AA, the Branch Post Offices at 24 Throgmorton Street, EC2N 2JE; 40 Fleet Street, EC4Y 1BT; 181 High Holborn, WC1 1AA; 2-4 Bishops Court, Chancery Lane, WC2A 1EA and from other large branch post offices in major towns and cities outside the Metropolitan Postal District as listed in form CAP 18 (which can be obtained from the Capital Taxes Office).

12

Printed in the UK for HMSO 1/89 Dd 8137979 250M 25038

For the purpose of this question the provisions of the Family Provision (Intestate Succession) Order 1987 (SI 1987/779) (ie increases in statutory legacies on intestacy with effect from 1 June 1987) should be ignored.

QUESTION 3

Document Provided: Oath for Executors

Meg Jenks, a Lecturer, of 1 Canal Street, Weytown, Surrey died on 1st July 1987 (aged 60), domiciled in England and Wales.

Her second husband, Bill, also of 1 Canal Street, survived her.

There were three children of Meg and Bill's marriage as follows:

1. Cyril, who died in 1986, leaving a widow, Tina and their two children, Daniel, two, and Fiona, born in 1987.
2. Albert (aged 22), who is married to Gillian. They have a daughter, Norma (one).
3. Patricia, who is 16 and married William West, on 30 June 1987.

Meg divorced her first husband, John Evans. He is still alive. The one child of their marriage, Hugh, died in 1980, survived by an unmarried daughter, Una, 17.

After her marriage to Bill, Meg made a will, appointing Bill her sole executor. In it she left him 'the balance on my bank account' (her sole property at that time). The will, which is valid, contains no further provisions.

Meg's estate is valued at £201,000 net of debts, and £209,000 gross at the date of her death. It consists of £30,000 in the bank account mentioned in the will, the remainder being quoted securities and personal chattels (the latter valued at £1,000.)

In August 1986 Meg gave the business which she owned to Albert. The business was then valued at £148,000. She had made no other lifetime gifts. Albert sold the business in May 1987 for £180,000.

(a) Disregarding any special rights Bill may have as surviving spouse, and Meg's gift of the business to Albert, set out who will be entitled to the estate, giving the precise nature of the respective entitlements, and stating what shares each beneficiary will or may take.

11 marks

(b) Disregarding factors of a tax nature, to what extent may

i) the income; and

ii) the capital

of their entitlement, if any, be paid to or applied for the benefit of Norma, Daniel, Fiona, Patricia and Una before they attain their respective majorities?

10 marks

(c) Albert dies intestate in 1988. He is survived by Gillian and Norma. He has had no more children. His net estate at death is £105,000, including personal chattels valued at £5,000. Norma dies in 1990, survived by Gillian.

Describe the entitlement as to both capital and income to Albert's estate

i) at his death;

8 marks ii) at Norma's death.

(d) Inheritance tax is payable on Meg's death.

So far as her personal representatives are concerned, will it be charged on £201,000? If you consider that inheritance tax will be charged on some other figure, give the figure involved, with your reasons for arriving at it. Tax calculations are not required.

9 marks

(e) In view of the gift to him and any relevant circumstances connnected with the gift, how, if at all, will Albert be affected as regards inheritance tax payable as a result of Meg's death?

If you consider that an inheritance tax liability arises in respect of the gift, explain how it will be calculated, giving your reasons.

Who is liable to pay any such tax?

3 marks Tax calculations themselves are not required.

(f) Complete the form of Oath supplied. No settled land is involved. The Oxford District Registry is to be used. Your firm, Smith & Co, 3 High Street, Weytown, are acting. Meg is not an alias.

5 marks

---

46 marks

Law Society Solicitors' Final Examination
Wills, Probate and Administration Summer 1987 Q2

QUESTION 3 - SOLUTION

General comment

The post-death question, for 46 marks, involved a detailed knowledge of the intestacy rules and their application in a fairly intricate setting. The well-prepared student, however, should not have experienced any difficulties. The subsidiary taxation aspects of the question were straightforward as was the Oath for Executors.

Suggested solution

a) There is a partial intestacy which has arisen under AEA 1925 because Meg's will fails to dispose of all her estate, she having left Bill nothing more than 'the balance on my bank account'. Entitlement to the estate, disregarding any special rights Bill might have (capitalisation of life-interest; appropriation of matrimonial home) is as follows:

   i) Bill will take the personal chattels, a statutory legacy of £75,000 and a life-interest in half the residue of the estate. However, Bill is required to make hotchpot of what he has received under the operative provisions of the will, namely the specific legacy of £30,000. This means he will only receive £45,000. Any income arising on the specific legacy until payment is due to him, together with interest upon the £45,000. John Evans, the first husband, not being 'a spouse', receives nothing.

   ii) Meg's children: there were four, and after the surviving spouse they are the next category of next-of-kin entitled, under s46 AEA. Their entitlement is in one-half of the residue held for them under the statutory trusts, that is to each child who attains 18, or marries under that age. Until then their interests are contingent. The issue are also entitled to the reversionary interest in the other half of residue expectant upon Bill's death, likewise on the statutory trusts of the AEA.

   Where a child predeceases the intestate, any issue who survive the intestate take per stirpes the share their parent would have taken, provided they attain 18 or marry under that age.

   Accordingly, Albert has a vested interest in possession in one-quarter of the issue's half share now available. He also has a vested interest in one-quarter of the reversionary element which will fall into possession on Bill's death. (The share amounts to one-quarter as Meg had four children.)

   Cyril predeceased his mother. The vesting of this share is contingent because if neither David nor Fiona attains 18, or marries below that age, that share will become divisible between Albert and Patricia (her interest being indefeasible because she has married) and Una, if she attains 18 or marries below that age. Therefore, Albert's share of the issue's share could itself grow to one-third, or one-half, but not larger because of Patricia's already vested interest. The same principle of quantum will apply to the reversion.

Daniel and Fiona are each entitled to one-half of the interest (in both the issue's fund and the reversion) which their parent Cyril would have taken provided respectively they attain 18 or marry earlier. Should one do so but the other fail to do so then the whole of that portion accrues to the one that does. Pat's entitlement is vested and therefore if she were now to die her estate would benefit. Una's interest remains contingent.

b) i) By virtue of s31 Trustee Act 1925, trustees may either apply income from a share of residue to which a child is contingently entitled for that child's maintenance education or benefit, or accumulate the income. This power is subject to any prior interest in the income: the trustees must consider what other funds are available from which income can be derived.

In applying these rules, Bill is entitled to the income of his fund for life. Only upon Bill's death will the income of that fund become available to the issue. Norma has no entitlement; Albert, her father, has survived Meg.

The trustees may apply one-eighth of the total issue's fund income for the benefit of Daniel and Fiona, or otherwise accumulate it for them.

As regards Patricia, being married she is already entitled to her share in the issue's fund and can give a valid receipt for the income.

The trustees may apply Una's income fund share for her benefit, or otherwise accumulate it for her.

In the event of the interest of Daniel, Fiona or Una failing to vest any income accumulations made for them would fall into the capital of the issue's fund and be divisible among those whose entitlements did vest.

ii) By s32 Trustee Act 1925 trustees are permitted to advance for an absolutely or contingently entitled beneficiary up to one-half of a vested or presumptive share. Where there is a prior life-interest in such share the life-tenant must give his written consent to such payment. As regards the reversion, Patricia has a vested interest but the trustees would only be able to make an advancement in Bill's lifetime with his written consent which is unlikely. She is, however, entitled to receive one-quarter of the issue's fund immediately.

Daniel, Fiona and Una may all be advanced up to half their contingent entitlement in the issue's fund if the trustees think fit and the same proportion of the reversion if Bill should agree.

c) i) As surviving spouse Gillian is entitled to the personal chattels, a statutory legacy of £75,000, with interest thereon until payment, and a life-interest in half the residue. The other half passes to Norma upon her attaining 18, or marrying earlier.

Albert's trustees may apply income, and up to one-half of Norma's contingent fund, subject to Gillian's consent, before her interest vests.

ii) Because Norma's interest was contingent upon her attaining 18, or marrying earlier, as to both capital and income her death will bring about the following consequences: Gillian will now be a surviving spouse without issue, but a parent of her late husband (Bill) may still be alive. If that is so, Gillian becomes entitled to the larger statutory legacy of £125,000, from which is deducted the £75,000 she will have received upon Albert's death. In addition, she receives half the residue, absolutely.

Bill is entitled to the remaining half, absolutely. However, if Bill does not survive Albert, Albert's brothers and sisters of the whole blood become entitled under the statutory trusts to the share Bill would have taken had he survived. The beneficiaries are therefore Cyril's children as to one-half, contingently, and Pat as to the other one-half; and the whole if neither of Cyril's children take.

d) Inheritance tax is payable upon the net estate of a deceased person, subject to exemptions and reliefs: in order to arrive at the rate to be charged the deceased's cumulative total of lifetime transferors has to be aggregated.

A transfer made by an individual to another, such as Meg's gift to Albert, is a Potentially Exempt Transfer. It becomes exempt and therefore never comes into the transferor's cumulative total if the transferor survives the making of the PET by seven years.

Business Property Relief (BPR) is available in respect of chargeable transfers of businesses meeting the conditions of the Relief. If this was such a business the effect would be to reduce the chargeable transfer by 50 per cent, and hence to reduce Meg's cumulative total. However, BPR is withdrawn where the donee sells the business, as is the case here. Thus, the full value of the gift, subject to the annual exemptions, will enter into Meg's cumulative total.

Transferors have available to them an annual exemption of £3,000, which may be deducted from transfers in arriving at their value for IHT. This exemption may be carried forward one year, if unused. Hence, the chargeable transfer amounts to £142,000. The tax is charged on the value at the time of the transfer, not upon the sale proceeds.

Meg's estate at death benefits her surviving spouse, absolutely as to chattels (£1,000) and as to statutory legacy of £75,000: he also takes a life-interest in half the residue. The remaining half of residue passes to Meg's issue. For IHT purposes a spouse's interest, whether absolute or limited, is exempt tax. Hence, only the issue's half is taxable.

Accordingly, inheritance tax will be calculated upon an £62,500 estate cumulated with the chargeable transfer of £142,000.

e) When Meg made the gift it was a PET. Albert is affected in two respects:

i) because the gift becomes chargeable as a result of Meg dying within seven years of it;

ii) because BPR has been withdrawn on account of Albert selling the business he now faces a liability because he is taxed on the full value at the time of the gift, and it therefore comes within taxable bands, after deducting the two years' annual exemptions. The primary person liable is Albert, but if he fails to pay within 12 months of the month of Meg's death, a secondary liability attaches to her PR's, up to the limit of the assets in her estate, whether or not they have by then distributed it.

f) Completed Oath for Executors (see pages 122-3).

Oath for Executors

IN THE HIGH COURT OF JUSTICE

Family Division

Extracting Solicitor Smith & Co.

Address 3, High Street, Weytown, Surrey

THE ~~PRINCIPAL REGISTRY~~ District Probate Registry at Oxford

IN the Estate of* Meg Jenks deceased.

(1) I, Bill Jenks of 1, Canal Street, Weytown, Surrey Lecturer

make Oath and say, (2) that

(1) I believe the paper writing now produced to and marked by (3) me to contain the true and original last Will and Testament (4)

of* Meg Jenks

of 1 Canal Street aforesaid

~~formerly of~~

deceased

who died on the 1st day of July 1987

aged 60 years (5) domiciled in (6) England and Wales

and that to the best of my knowledge, information and belief there was (7) [no] land vested in the said deceased which was settled previously to her death (and not by her Will (4))

and which remained settled land notwithstanding her death (8)

~~And I/we further make oath and say (2) that notice of this application has been given to~~

~~the executor(s) to whom power is to be reserved,~~ [save]. (9)

*If necessary to include alias of deceased in grant add "otherwise (alias name)" and state below which is true name and reason for requiring alias.

(1) "I" *or* "We". Insert the full name, place of residence and occupation or, if none, description of the deponent(s), adding "Mrs", "Miss", as appropriate, for a female deponent.

(2) *Or* "do solemnly and sincerely affirm".

(3) Each testamentary paper must be marked by each deponent, and by the person administering the oath.

(4) "with one, two (or more) Codicils", as the case may be.

(5) If exact age is unknown, give best estimate.

(6) Where there are separate legal divisions in one country, the state, province, etc., should be specified.

(7) Delete "no", if there was land vested in deceased which remained settled land notwithstanding his death.

(8) Settled land may be included in the scope of the grant provided the executors are also the special executors as to the settled land; in that case the settlement must be identified.

(9) Delete or amend as appropriate. Notice of this application must be served on all executors to whom power is to be reserved unless dispensed with by a registrar under Rule 27 (3).

(10) "I am" *or* "we are". Insert relationship of the executors to the deceased only if necessary to establish title or identification.

(11) "The sole", *or* "the surviving", *or* "one of the", *or* "are the", *or* "two of the", etc.

(12) If there was settled land and the grant is to include it, insert "including settled land" but, if the grant is to exclude the settled land, insert "save and except settled land".

(13) Complete this paragraph only if the deceased died on or after 1 April 1981 and an Inland Revenue Account is not required; the next paragraph should be deleted.

(14) Insert "100,000" in respect of deaths on or after 1 April 1989, "70,000 in respect of deaths on or after 1 April 1987, "40,000" in respect of deaths on or after 1 April 1983 or "25,000" in respect of deaths prior to that date.

(15) Insert currently "10,000", "25,000", "40,000", "70,000", or "100,000" as appropriate.

(16) Complete this paragraph only if an Inland Revenue Account is required and delete the previous paragraph.

N.B. The names of all executors to whom power is to be reserved must be included in the Oath.

And (1) I further make Oath and say (2) that (10) (11) I am the sole Executor named in the said will

and that (1) I will (i) collect, get in and administer according to the law the real and personal estate (12) of the said deceased; (ii) when required to do so by the Court, exhibit on oath in the Court a full inventory of the said estate (12) and when so required render an account of the administration of the said estate to the Court; and (iii) when required to do so by the High Court, deliver up the grant of probate to that Court; and that to the best of my knowledge, information and belief

(13) [the gross estate passing under the grant does not exceed (14) £ , and the net estate does not exceed (15) £ , and that this is not a case in which an Inland Revenue Account is required to be delivered]

(16) [the gross estate passing under the grant amounts to £ 209,000 and the net estate amounts to £ 201,000].

SWORN by Bill Jenks the above-named Deponent

at

this day of 19 ,

Before me, A. Bloggs (independent solicitor)

A Commissioner for Oaths/Solicitor.

QUESTION 4

Document Provided: Oath for Administrators with the will

You are an assistant solicitor with Smith & Co of 3 Canal Street, Chesterfield, Derbyshire. Your reference is W.

You receive instructions to obtain a grant of representation in the estate of Albert Cromford, who died on 10 January 1988. He was unmarried and lived at 11 Cross Street, Chesterfield. He is survived by his parents, John and Ethel Cromford, and by his unmarried sister, Susan, aged 30. He was domiciled in England and Wales.

Albert was born on 30 March 1960 and, like his father, was a builder.

You are to use the Manchester District Probate Registry.

John, Ethel and Susan all live at 50 Cross Street, Chesterfield.

His estate comprises:	**Assets**	**Value £**
	Accounts with Allbank PLC (outside his business):	
	Current Account	2,500
	Deposit Account including interestaccrued to date of death	30,000
	Quoted stocks, shares and other investments	120,000
	Personal belongings - estimated value	10,000
	Business - estimated value (net of business debts)	100,000
	11 Cross Street - estimated value	50,000
	Liabilities (outside the business) including the funeral account - estimated at £2,000	

Albert left a short home made will, which you may assume is valid, as follows:

'1. This is the last will of me Albert Cromford

2. I give my personal belongings to my friend Herbert Smith

3. I give all my other property to my sister

(Signed) Albert Cromford (Dated) 30th December 1986.

(Signed) James Green Susan Cromford'

Albert had made one lifetime transfer only: in December 1986 he gave his sister a cottage then worth £20,000. At his death, through increase in local property values, the cottage had an estimated value of £30,000.

(a) Explain:

(i) who is primarily entitled to a grant of representation;

(ii) who else is entitled if the person referred to in your answer to (a)(i) is unable or unwilling to act;

9 marks (iii) who is entitled to Albert's residuary estate.

(b) Complete the form of Oath supplied on the basis that whoever is named by you in your answer to (a) (i) proves the will.

6 marks No settled land is involved.

(c) Give details of any specific inheritance tax rules applying to the various assets of Albert's estate which affect either:

(i) valuation of the asset during the administration period (including at death); or

7 marks (ii) the manner in which the tax applicable to the relevant asset may be paid.

(d) How, if at all, will the gift of the cottage affect the liability of Albert's personal representative(s) to inheritance tax on Albert's estate?

Include in your answer an explanation of how the value of the cottage will be arrived at for the computation of the tax liability, if you consider that the gift is relevant for inheritance tax purposes as at

8 marks Albert's death.

(e) Because of a fall in property values, the property 11 Cross Street is sold on the open market at £40,000 (before the deduction of sale expenses) in June 1989 and during the administration of the estate.

Advise the personal representative(s) as to:

(i) how, if at all, this may affect their inheritance tax liability and the manner in which the tax could be paid;

(ii) in the light of your answer to (e)(i), their capital gains tax position regarding the sale of the property;

(iii) the difference in the effect of these two taxes had the property been sold in June 1989 for £60,000 (before deduction of sale expenses).

11 marks

41 marks

Law Society Solicitors' Final Examination
Wills, Probate and Administration Winter 1988 Q2

QUESTION 4 - SOLUTION

General comment

This question concentrated heavily on administration and taxation aspects of the syllabus and, on the whole, was fairly testing, although by no means unfair: generally, a satisfactory question which may have separated the wheat among the candidates from the chaff.

Suggested solution

a) i) Entitlement to a grant of representation to the estate of Albert Cromford will be determined by application of Non-Contentions Probate Rules, as Albert left a will but did not leave proving executors.

Accordingly, grant of representation will issue to the ultimate residuary legatee and devisee, in the absence of anyone in higher rank. This means that grant of administration with the will annexed issues in principle to Albert's sister, Susan Cromford. However, Susan has witnessed the will and as there is no supernumerary witness, it appears that Susan will lose the benefit of her residuary entitlement: s15 Wills Act 1837.

ii) In the event, Susan having lost her right to entitlement, administration with will annexed issues to Albert's parents, equally. NCPRs states that ' ... where the residue is not wholly disposed of by the will any person entitled to share in the residue not so disposed of ...' (is entitled). Accordingly, John and Ethel Cromford, because they will take under the partial intestacy which arises, may be entitled. On another view, it can be argued that the residue has been wholly disposed of but fails for extraneous reasons - Susan's witnessing of the will - and that therefore Hubert Smith, ranking as a specific legatee, would be entitled. The better view is that John and Ethel will take out a grant.

iii) Albert's residuary estate now lapses and passes under a partial intestacy. Being unmarried and having therefore neither surviving spouse, nor issue, Albert's estate passes to the next entitled persons, that is, his parents John and Ethel Cromford, in equal shares.

b) Completed Oath for Administrators with the will (see pages 130-1).

c) i) The valuation of the current account and deposit account, which includes interest accrued to date of death, presents no difficulties. Their value at death will be shown in the Inland Revenue Account.

The quoted stocks and shares will be valued at one-quarter up from the lower of the two prices quoted in the Stock Exchange Official list at the date of death. This is the recognised probate practice. If the shares are valued 'cum div' it means that the share has been calculated on the basis that a purchaser buying the stocks or shares would be entitled to the whole of the next dividend. The share price is therefore increased to compensate the vendor for the loss of that part of the year's interest or dividend that has already accrued. For inheritance tax purposes if the probate valuation is made 'cum div' that value is entered on the Inland Revenue Account, no further reference being made to the dividend, since the value of the dividend or interest is included in the share price. For inheritance tax purposes if the probate valuation is made 'ex div' the 'ex div' price is entered on the Inland Revenue account and so is the whole of the dividend payment which will be paid to the estate by the company.

ii) As to the manner in which the tax applicable to the relevant asset may be paid, the bank accounts, quoted stocks shares and other investments and personal belongings will be entered in the Inland Revenue Account in section 1A inheritance tax on these assets, less the liabilities, will be assessed in the appropriate bands of tax and the tax paid on delivery of the account: there will be no instalment option available.

With regard to the business and the property, 11 Cross Street, these assets will be entered in section 1B, and the inheritance tax attributable thereto may be paid by the personal representatives in ten yearly instalments, if they so elect. When the asset is realised and becomes personalty the tax falls due: interest becomes payable at the rate of 9 per cent on tax outstanding from six months after the end of the month of death.

d) Inheritance tax is payable upon the net estate of a deceased person, subject to exemptions and reliefs: in order to arrive at the rate to be charged the deceased's cumulative total of lifetime transfers has to be aggregated. A transfer made by an individual to another, such as Albert Cromford's transfer in December 1986 to his sister Susan, is a potentially exempt transfer at the time it is made: it would have become exempt and therefore never come into the transferor's cumulative total if Albert had survived the making of the PET by seven years. In the event, Albert has died 13 months after making the gift of the cottage.

Inheritance tax is always a 'progressive' tax in that the rate of tax increases as the total of taxable gifts made by the transferor increases: in order to establish what rate of tax is to be charged on a particular chargeable transfer account will have to be taken of all previous chargeable transfer made by the transferor within the previous seven years.

The transfer occasioned by Albert's death will be added, therefore, to the transfer of the cottage to Susan and the inheritance tax will then be calculated as if the present transfer is the highest part and so taxed at the highest rate of a single transfer equal to all the transfers made within the last seven years.

e) i) If a deceased was entitled to an interest in land at the time of death and that interest is sold for less than the market value at death the personal representatives can claim to have the sale price substituted for the market value at death, provided the sale takes place within three years of death.

Conversely, as possibly here, the Revenue have power to substitute the best consideration that could reasonably have been obtained on the sale if this is higher than the sale price.

Property values have fallen and the property is sold during the administration period 18 months after death. The likelihood is that in the circumstances the personal representatives' liability will be unaffected. However, the manner in which the tax is paid will be affected in so far as the tax attributable to the instalment option falls due and the personal representatives become accountable.

ii) & iii)

There is no charge to capital gains tax on death. The deceased's assets are acquired by the personal representatives for a consideration equal to market value at the date of death. Where the personal representatives, as here, sell assets in the course of administration they become liable to CGT only on the difference between the sale consideration and market value at the deceased's death, with deduction for any allowable expenditure and indexation allowance, including an appropriate proportion of the cost of obtaining the grant of representation. They can offset any capital losses against their chargeable gains in the year of assessment, carrying forward any excess losses to the next year. They have the benefit of the individual's yearly exempt amount for the year of assessment in which the deceased died and for the two following years, after which their chargeable gains are taxed at 25 per cent. (Any losses unrelieved at the end of the administration of the estate cannot be transferred to the beneficiaries.)

If the property had been sold in June 1989 for £60,000 (before deduction of sale expenses) for IHT purposes there would be no difference in so far as the Revenue would probably accept that the increase in value of £10,000 represented a true value 18 months after death.

Turn over for completed Oath for Administrators with the will, question 4(b).

Oath for Administrators with the Will

IN THE HIGH COURT OF JUSTICE

Family Division

Extracting Solicitor Smith & Co (Ref W)

Address 3, Canal Street, Chesterfield, Derbyshire

The ~~Principal Registry~~ District Registry at Manchester

IN the Estate of* Albert Cromford deceased.

(1) We, John Cromford and Ethel Cromford, both of 50, Cross Street, Chesterfield, Derbyshire

make Oath and say (2) that

(1) we believe the paper writing now produced to and marked by (3) us to contain the true and original last Will and Testament (4)

of* Albert Cromford

of 11, Cross Street, Chesterfield aforesaid

~~formerly of~~

deceased,

who died on the 10th day of January 1988

aged 27 years (5) domiciled in (6) England and Wales

and that (7) no minority and (7) no life interest in the estate of the said deceased; and that to the best of our knowledge, information and belief there was (8) [no] land vested in the deceased which was settled previously to his death (and not by his Will (4)) and which remained settled land notwithstanding his death (9)

*If necessary to include alias of deceased in grant, add "otherwise (alias name)" and state below which is true name and reason for requiring alias.

(1) "I" *or* "We". Insert the full name, place of residence and occupation or, if none, description of the deponent(s) adding "Mrs." "Miss", as appropriate, for a female deponent.

(2) *Or* "do solemnly and sincerely affirm".

(3) Each testamentary paper must be marked by each deponent, and by the person administering the oath.

(4) "With one, two (or more) Codicils", as the case may be.

(5) If exact age is unknown, give best estimate.

(6) Where there are separate legal divisions in one country, the state, province, etc., should be stated.

(7) Complete both blanks. When either such interest arises, two grantees may be required unless a trust corporation is applying.

(8) Delete "no", if there was settled land vested in deceased which remained settled land notwithstanding his death.

(9) If there was settled land such land may be included in the scope of the grant, but the settlement must be identified and all the applicants must show that they are also entitled to a grant in respect of the settled land.

(10) Here state manner in which all prior rights are satisfied, e.g., residuary legatees/devisees must show that no executors were appointed, or that those appointed either died before

deceased or survived him and have since died without taking probate, or that they have renounced probate, or have failed to take a grant after being cited so to do (*the order authorising a grant to citor being quoted*).

(11) "I am" or "we are" and state title of applicants to the grant, including their relationship to the deceased only if necessary to establish title or identification.

(12) If there was settled land and the grant is to include it, insert "including settled land", but, if the grant is to exclude the settled land, insert "save and except settled land".

(13) Complete this paragraph only if the deceased died on or after 1 April 1981 and an Inland Revenue Account is not required; the next paragraph should be deleted.

(14) Insert "70,000" in respect of deaths on or after 1 April 1987, "40,000" in respect of deaths on or after 1 April 1983, or "25,000" in respect of deaths prior to that date.

(15) Insert currently "10,000" "25,000", "40,000", or "70,000" as appropriate.

(16) Complete this paragraph only if an Inland Revenue Account is required and delete the previous paragraph.

and (1) we further make Oath and say (2)
that (10) the deceased died testate without appointing executors and the residuary beneficiary Susan Crawford has lost her entitlement to the residue by witnessing the will and
that (11) we are the lawful parents of the deceased and the persons first entitled in equal shares to the undisposed of estate,

; and that

(1) We will (i) collect, get in and administer according to the law the real and personal Estate (12) of the said deceased; (ii) when required to do so by the Court, exhibit on oath in the Court a full inventory of the said Estate, (12) and when so required render an account of the administration of the said Estate to the Court; and (iii) when required to do so by the High Court deliver up the grant of letters of administration with Will annexed to that Court; and that to the best of our knowledge, information and belief.

(13) [the gross estate passing under the grant does not exceed (14) £ , and the net estate does not exceed (15) £ , and that this is not a case in which an Inland Revenue Account is required to be delivered]

(16) [the gross estate passing under the grant amounts to £312,500 and the net estate amounts to £ 310,500].
*

SWORN by the above-named Deponents
John Crawford
Susan Crawford

at 1, Vicarage Road, Chesterfield

this 15th day of February 1988

Before me, (independent solicitor)
A Commissioner for Oaths/Solicitor.

QUESTION 5

Document Provided: Oath for Administrators

Gerald Green died intestate on 1 June 1988 at his home 21 North Street, Sutton, Southshire. He was of English domicile.

Gerald was survived by his widow, Joan. There were two children of the marriage: Charles (who died in July 1986) and Fiona (now aged 17). Gerald also had a third child, Herbert (30), by his mistress, Elizabeth Broad.

Charles was survived by two children, Susan and Ian; his wife, Wendy, predeceased him. Susan (21) is married to Fred Brown and they have one child, Tom (two).

Ian died in November 1987 survived by his widow, Martha, and the two children of their marriage: Eileen (one) and Norman (born on 15 June 1988).

Fiona married Michael White in May 1988. They have no children.

Gerald's death certificate shows Gerald's name as Gerald Edward Green. This is also the name shown on his birth certificate. However, the family say that he was always known as Gerald Green. All his assets were held in the name of Gerald Edward Green except the house at 21 North Street: the conveyance of this property, which was the matrimonial home of Gerald and Joan, vested it in the sole name of Gerald Green.

The total value of Gerald's estate is £350,000 net of debts. It includes quoted shares, which although worth £60,000 at death have been falling in value since and are now only worth £30,000. Stockbrokers advise that they have gone down about as far as is likely. They also say that little recovery can be expected in the forseeable future.

Gerald's mistress, Elizabeth, was partly maintained by him for some two years before the birth of their child, Herbert, until Gerald died.

(a) On the assumption that Joan does not exercise any special rights she may have in her capacity as surviving spouse, who if those mentioned will be entitled to share in the estate? Explain in what manner and in what shares they will be so entitled. **12 marks**

(b) Explain fully, by reference to any relevant statutory provisions, the extent to which either the capital or income of their entitlement may be applied for the benefit of any of those entitled who are minors, before they reach majority. **5 marks**

(c) Explain any special rights available to Joan in her capacity as surviving spouse and when she may exercise them. **3 marks**

(d) Assume (for the purpose of this part question only) that Gerald gave Charles £4,000 on Charles's marriage. What effect, if any, would this have on your answer to (a)? **3 marks**

(e) What rights might Elizabeth Broad have to share in Gerald's estate? How should any such rights be asserted and on what grounds? Towards establishing what points should any case to be made by Elizabeth be directed? How could the personal representatives be protected from such a claim? **7 marks**

(f) Assume (for the purpose of this part question only) that there is uncertainty about Herbert; that the family have had no contact with him for some ten years; that he was last heard of in Wales; that he may even have died leaving children surviving. In these circumstances what would you suggest should be done to deal with this situation in the administration of the estate? **11 marks**

(g) Who do you consider would be entitled to take out the grant? What is the effect of the grant and what authority does the administrator have before its issue? Any differences between the authority of an administrator and an executor should be mentioned. **7 marks**

(h) (i) When is inheritance tax normally due and payable in relation to a deceased's estate?

(ii) Will any inheritance tax payable be calculated on the basis of a value of £350,000 or otherwise?

(iii) Explain in what circumstances the payment of inheritance tax may in this case be reduced and/or deferred.

Note: (A) Do not attempt to calculate the amount of any inheritance tax that may be due.

(B) Assume that there have been no lifetime chargeable or potentially exempt transfers. **12 marks**

(i) Using the Southtown District Probate Registry, complete the Oath for Administrators supplied. The extracting solicitor should be shown as ABS (reference X) of Bank House, Southtown. If there are any matters on which you need further instructions in order to complete the form you should indicate this on the form, but please do not complete the jurat. **8 marks**

---

68 marks

Law Society Solicitors' Final Examination
Wills, Probate and Administration Summer 1988 Q1

QUESTION 5 - SOLUTION

General comment

This was a detailed question on intestacy involving application of the rules as to entitlement and the special rights available to a surviving spouse. It also involved knowledge of the statutory advertisement procedure and family provision: unfortunately Question 5(e) was badly worded and may have confused many students. On the whole a good question, although it must be said that question-spotters are having a field day in this subject in that, very understandably, the examiner is running out of new themes. Within the constraints of the examination system there is little that can be done to overcome this phenomenon until the structure of the examination is altered.

Suggested solution

a) Entitlement to the estate of Joan rests on the intestacy rules, set down in s33 Administration of Estates 1925, which provides for a statutory trust for sale of all undisposed of property vesting in the deceased's personal representatives.

The order of distribution is governed by s46 AEA. Gerald has left surviving spouse and issue. Joan will take:

i) personal chattels, as defined by s55 (1)(x) AEA, absolutely;

ii) a statutory legacy of £75,000, free of tax, and with interest thereon from date of death until payment;

iii) a life interest in half the remainder of the residuary estate.

The balance of the estate, comprising one half of the residue and the reversionary element in Joan's life interest, will be held on the statutory trusts for Gerald's issue.

The statutory trusts are set out in s47 AEA. The property is held equally for the children of the intestate who are either alive or en ventre sa mére at the date of the intestate's death. Such child or children take a contingent interest unless and until they reach 18 years or marry under that age: if a child predeceases the intestate leaving issue at the date of death, those grandchildren will take per stirpes the share their parent would have taken provided they reach 18 or marry under that age.

Applying these rules those prima-facie entitled are Herbert, the issue of Charles and Fiona. Herbert has attained 18 and so takes a vested one-third interest. Although illegitimate, Herbert is entitled because an illegitimate may succeed to either of his parents' estates as if he were legitimate because, in respect of deaths occurring after 4 April 1988, the distribution of assets is to be determined without regard to whether or not the parents were married to each other - see Family Law Reform Act 1987.

Fiona is married and so her interest in one-third is also vested.

Susan, Eileen and Norman take per stirpes the share Charles would have taken. Susan is entitled to a vested one-sixth share; Eileen and Norman have a contingent one-twelfth share each upon the statutory trusts of the AEA, as their father, Ian, predeceased the intestate. Norman's entitlement rests on his being en ventre sa mére at the intestate's death. If both Eileen and Norman were to die unmarried under 18, Susan would take the whole of Charles's one-third share; if either Eileen or Norman satisfied the statutory trusts, but the other did not, the whole one-sixth share would then accrue to the one that did.

b) Joan has a life interest in half the residue. Subject thereto, the income and half the capital of the respective shares of Eileen and Norman may be applied during their minorities for their benefit, in accordance with ss31 and 32 Trustee Act 1925.

Fiona is a married minor. She can give a good receipt for income but not for capital - s21 Law of Property Act 1925. This means that until she attains 18 the capital will be held on trust for Fiona by the personal representatives.

Under s31 Trustee Act, the trustees holding property for a minor may apply the income of the property, subject to the prior interest, for the purposes of maintenance, education and benefit. Under s32 Trustee Act 1925, where a beneficiary has an interest in trust capital the trustees may apply up to one-half of the vested or presumptive share of that capital for the purposes of advancement or benefit, subject to the written consent of any person with a prior interest - in this case Joan.

c) The special rights available to Joan must be exercised within 12 months of the grant of representation to Gerald's estate. They are:

i) to redeem the life-interest for a lump sum of capital: s47A AEA 1925. The election to redeem must be in writing and will mean substitution of capital for income.

ii) to take the matrimonial home as part of any absolute entitlement under the intestacy, including the capitalised life interest. The house is valued at the date of appropriation and not the date of death.

d) If Gerald gave Charles £4,000 a question of hotchpot would be raised, a presumption being made that a parent would wish to treat his children equally. The payment would be subject to the rules contained in s47(1)(iii) AEA, provided that it was made either on the marriage of the child (Charles) or by way of advancement. Here the former applies. Accordingly, the £4,000 would have to be brought into account in calculating the amount due to those entitled through Charles: Susan, Eileen and Norman.

e) Elizabeth Broad has no rights to any beneficial entitlement under the intestacy since she does not come within the statutory order of s46 AEA. She may, however, be able to assert a claim under the Inheritance (Provision for Family and Dependants) Act 1975, as a person who, immediately before the death of the deceased, was being wholly or partly maintained by him, otherwise than for full valuable consideration: s1(1)(e) 1975 Act.

The word 'maintained' means the making of a substantial contribution in money or money's worth towards Elizabeth's reasonable needs: s1(3).

The claim would be made under s2 of the Act on the basis that the law of intestacy fails to make adequate provision for her maintenance. The court would pay regard to Elizabeth's own resources, the size and nature of the estate, the fact that she appears to have been partly maintained by Gerald for 32 years, her conduct and any statement of reasons left by the deceased. The needs and resources of other beneficiaries would also be a relevant consideration and the court would look at the position not only at the date of death but also at the date of the hearing.

The personal representatives could protect themselves by waiting for six months from grant of representation before making any distribution. If they do that and no claim is made they will be protected. The court may in its discretion extend this six-month period but the PR's are not deemed to have constructive knowledge of any such extended time.

The property may nevertheless be recovered from a beneficiary under the normal equitable rules of tracing.

A personal representative cannot be protected merely because statutory advertisements have been placed under s27 Trustee Act 1925 to which no response has been forthcoming within the period of two months.

f) In the circumstances the personal representatives should make as many personal enquiries of people who may have been expected to have had contact with Herbert: his family, friends, professional or business colleagues. Having exhausted this line of enquiry (or at the same time) the personal representatives should advertise for information as to Herbert's whereabouts in newspapers circulating in the district where he was last heard of.

If Herbert does not respond the personal representatives may apply to the court for a 'Benjamin' order declaring that they be at liberty to distribute the estate on the footing that Herbert predeceased without leaving issue.

Alternatively, the PR's may seek an indemnity from the other beneficiaries, although a difficulty here is that two of them are minors and could not validly join in. Insurance could be taken out to cover any prospective liability which the PR's may incur.

The statutory advertisement procedure under s27 Trustee Act 1925 would be exercised as a matter of course but it would be of no real value on these facts because it only provides protection against such claims of which the PR's have no notice and here they do know of Herbert's existence and his potential claim, even though he cannot be located at present.

Nevertheless, the statutory advertisement procedure would protect the PR's against any other possible beneficiaries or creditors.

g) Entitlement to a grant will be determined by NCPRs. Letters of administration will issue to one or more of the persons of full age interested in the residuary estate if they make application for the purpose.

In order of priority comes Joan, as surviving spouse, and the children and issue of any child who has predeceased Gerald. The relevant persons of full age are Herbert and Susan. So Joan, Herbert or Susan may apply: although the court has discretion to appoint a sole administrator, where there is a minority or life interest, if it appears to the court to be expedient in all the circumstances, normally two or a trust corporation will be required.

A grant of letters of administration confers upon the grantee the required authority, whereas executors derive their authority from the will and the grant of probate is merely confirmatory of their powers.

h) i) Inheritance tax is due six months after the end of the month of death. It is payable upon delivery of the Inland Revenue Account, which itself must be delivered within 12 months after the end of the month of death. It will not be possible to obtain a grant until the inheritance tax payable on delivery of the account has been paid. Unpaid inheritance tax is liable to interest from the date when it is due, again, subject only to qualification where instalment relief applies: interest is not deductible for the purpose of income tax.

ii) IHT is calculated on the net value of the estate for tax purposes - ie the value of all the property to which the deceased was beneficially entitled (not including, however, excluded property) less debts and liabilities to the extent they were incurred for a consideration in money or money's worth or if imposed by law.

The figure of £350,000 will be reduced by such reliefs as are available, including here the surviving spouse exemption: the nil rate band of £128,000 can be utilised as well. Joan's rights as spouse will be the value at death of everything to which she is entitled and, so far as the life interest is concerned, it will be the capital value that will be brought into account.

iii) Inheritance tax may in this case be reduced by substituting a lower value for that obtaining at death. Once the grant has been obtained this can be done with the quoted shares which qualify for loss on sale relief; if sold within 12 months of death the sale price may be substituted for the value at death. A refund of tax, and any interest paid, may be obtained. Clearly there is scope for reduction in this way.

The burden may be mitigated by exercising the right to pay tax by instalments. This right applies to the house only on the facts of this question (no indication of there being a company which gave the deceased control, or to unquoted shares). The right is to pay by ten yearly instalments the first of which is payable on the date when the tax would otherwise be payable.

If the house is sold before all tax has been paid the outstanding balance becomes due. Interest will be payable on the outstanding IHT regardless of the right to pay by instalments.

i) Completed Oath for Administrators (see pages 138-9).

Oath for Administrators

IN THE HIGH COURT OF JUSTICE

Family Division

Extracting Solicitor ABC (Ref X)

Address Bank House, Southtown

The ~~Principal Registry~~ District Probate Registry at Southtown

IN the Estate of* Gerald Edward Green (otherwise Gerald Green) deceased.

(1) We, Joan Green of 21 North Street, Sutton, Southshire, widow and Herbert Green [or Susan] of [address required]

make Oath and say (2)

that* Gerald Edward Green (otherwise Gerald Green)

of 21, North Street, Sutton, Southshire

deceased,

died on the 1st day of June 1988

aged [required] years (3) domiciled in (4) England and Wales

Intestate (5)

~~(6) or any other person entitled in priority to share in h estate by virtue of any enactment~~ and that (7) a minority (7) and a life interest arises under the intestacy; and that to the best of our knowledge, information and belief there was (8) [no] land vested in the said deceased which was settled previously to his death and which remained settled land notwithstanding his death (9)

*If necessary to include alias of deceased in grant, add "otherwise (alias name)" and state below which is true name and reason for requiring alias.

(1) "I" *or* "We". Insert the full name, place of residence and occupation or, if none, description of the deponent(s) adding "Mrs." "Miss", as appropriate, for a female deponent.

(2) *or* "do so solemnly and sincerely affirm".

(3) If exact age is unknown, give best estimate.

(4) Where there are separate legal divisions in one country, the state, province, etc., should be stated.

(5) Here give the status of deceased–"a spinster", "a widower", etc., and where necessary clear off the classes entitled in order of priority to applicant, e.g., "without issue or parent".

(6) The words which follow clear illegitimate, legitimated and adopted children and should be deleted if application made by surviving spouse (unless in the special circumstances it is necessary to clear issue) or a child. If appropriate substitute "without" for "or".

(7) Complete both blanks. When either such interest arises two grantees may be required unless a trust corporation is applying.

(8) Delete "no", if there was land vested in deceased which remained settled land

notwithstanding his death.

(9) If there was settled land such land may be included in the scope of the grant, but the settlement must be identified and all the applicants must show that they are also entitled to a grant in respect of the settled land.

(10) "I am" or "we are".

(11) Show applicant's title, e.g., "brother of the whole blood and one of the persons entitled to share in the estate".

(12) If there was settled land and the grant is to include it, insert "including settled land", but, if the grant is to exclude the settled land, insert "save and except settled land".

(13) Complete this paragraph only if the deceased died on or after 1 April 1981 and an Inland Revenue Account is not required; the next paragraph should be deleted.

(14) Insert "100,000" in respect of deaths on or after 1 April 1989, "70,000" in respect of deaths on or after 1 April 1987, "40,000" in respect of deaths on or after 1 April 1983, or "25,000" in respect of deaths prior to that date.

(15) Insert currently "10,000", "25,000", "40,000", "70,000", or "100,000" as appropriate.

(16) Complete this paragraph only if an Inland Revenue Account is required and delete the previous paragraph.

And (1) we further make Oath and say (2) that (10) I the (11) said Joan Green am the lawful widow and relict of the deceased and that I Herbert Green am the [natural] son of the deceased and we are two of the persons entitled to share in the estate of the said Intestate,

and that (1) we will (i) collect, get in and administer according to the law the real and personal Estate (12) of the said deceased; (ii) when required to do so by the Court, exhibit on oath in the Court a full inventory of the said Estate (12) and when so required render an account of the administration of the said Estate to the Court; and (iii) when required to do so by the High Court, deliver up the grant of letters of administration to that Court; and that to the best of our knowledge, information and belief

~~(13) [the gross estate passing under the grant does not exceed (14) £ , and the net estate does not exceed (15) £ , and that this is not a case in which an Inland Revenue Account is required to be delivered]~~

(16) [the gross estate passing under the grant amounts to £ [required] and the net estate amounts to £ 350,000].

* That the true name of the deceased was Gerald Edward Green and that he held the property, 21 North Street, Sutton in the name of Gerald Green

SWORN by the above-named Deponent Joan Green Herbert Green [or Susan]

at

this day of 19

Before me, (an independent solicitor)

A Commissioner for Oaths/Solicitor.

QUESTION 6

Document Provided: Inland Revenue Account (IHT 200)

WYZ Solicitors act for the executors of William Shaw. The deceased a widower with one adult child. John, was a company director. WYZ's reference is ST and their address South House, Brampton, Cleveland.

To enable them to obtain a grant of probate in the Newcastle District Registry, WYZ have obtained the following information.

(1) Deceased, William Shaw, born 20 October 1928; died 30 November 1988; address 3 Broadway, Brampton; domiciled in England and Wales.

(2) Sole executor John Shaw of 32 Tyne Street, Durham.

(3) Apart from a legacy of £20,000 to the Laing Art Gallery, Newcastle, the estate is given to John absolutely.

(4) No nominations; no joint property.

(5) Lifetime gifts:

Date	Beneficiary	Amount
		£
1 July 1986	John	50,000 (cash)
1 December 1987	John	50,000 (cash)
1 May 1988	Aunt Agatha Brown	60,000 (house)

The value of the house at William Shaw's death was £80,000.

(6) William Shaw was life tenant of the trust created by the will of his wife, Elizabeth, who died on 1 July 1986. Details of the trust at the death of William Shaw are:

(i)	Assets	£
	Stock Exchange investments	65,000
	Cash capital net of accrued liabilities	35,000

(ii) The remainderman is John, who is the sole trustee.

(iii) Capital Taxes Office reference: F678/1986

(7) William Shaw's assets:

	£
Midland Bank, Brampton: Current Account	30,000
House: 3 Broadway	50,000
House contents (unsold)	2,000
Private car (unsold)	28,000

Unquoted shares in two family manufacturing companies:

(i) 6,500 ordinary shares of £1 cash in F Ltd (65 per cent of the voting shares)	100,000
(ii) 3,000 ordinary shares of £1 each in P Ltd (20 per cent of the voting shares)	3,000
Shaw Farm, near Brampton	400,000

(freehold owned by the deceased since 1980 and let by him to an agricultural tenant throughout the period of ownership)

Liabilities:

Tax due to date of death (estimated)	9,000
Funeral (C & Co)	1,000

(8) Insurance policy

Effected 1983 by William Shaw. It provides £100,000 payable on William Shaw's death, written in trust for John, absolutely, John is trustee of the policy. Premiums paid; £2,500 per annum.

(a) Please draft the Inland Revenue Account (Form IHT 200 supplied), except Pages 11 and 12. You should provide a schedule of chargeable gifts by setting one out in your answer book. **20 marks**

(b) To what extent is it possible to pay the inheritance tax (IHT) arising on the deceased's death by instalments? Where this is possible, specify the asset involved. State in each case whether or not the instalments, if paid immediately they fall due, will bear interest. **7 marks**

(c) Apart from assets specified in paragraph (7), on whom does the liability to pay IHT fall?

If you consider that any liability arises in the case of the gift made in 1988, how should XYZ advise John? He tells them that Aunt Agatha has sold the house and dissipated the proceeds. **8 marks**

(d) Advise John from what sources he should consider raising the funds to pay the IHT. Explain the factors you would take into account in choosing between possible sources of funds.

Calculations are not required. **8 marks**

---

43 marks

Adapted from Law Society Solicitors' Final Examination
Wills, Probate and Administration Winter 1989 Q2

QUESTION 6 - SOLUTION

General comment

Again a fairly standard post-death question and the issues of payment of tax by instalments and raising the money to pay the tax due have been asked many times before. The IHT form was a more complicated one than usual.

Suggested solution

a) Schedule of chargeable gifts

Date of gift	*Donee*	*Gross amount*	*Exemptions claimed*	*Net amount*
1/7/1986	John Shaw	£50,000	1986/87 £3,000	£44,000
			1985/86 £3,000	
1/12/1987	John Shaw	£50,000	1987/88 £3,000	£47,000
1/5/1988	Aunt Agatha	£60,000	1988/89 £3,000	£57,000

Completed IHT form 200 (see pages 144-163). Note: pages 11 and 12 of IHT form 200 are not required for this question. For examples of pages 11 and 12, see suggested solution to question 2 earlier in this chapter.

b) As the executor John Shaw has an option to pay tax in ten yearly instalments on certain assets with the first instalment falling due six months after the end of the month of death. The instalment option is available on land (the house 3 Broadway and Shaw Farm) and shares which gave the deceased control of a company (the 65 per cent holding in F Ltd). The instalment option would only be available on the shares in P Ltd if the Revenue were satisfied that payment of the tax in one lump sum would cause 'undue hardship' and this is unlikely on the facts.

In the event of late payment interest will be charged on the outstanding instalment and in the case of land which is not a business asset and shares in investment companies interest will be charged on the total outstanding IHT liability (even if the instalments are paid on time). If the asset subject to the instalment option is sold the outstanding instalments become due at once.

c) The lifetime gifts were potentially exempt transfers when they were made but they have become taxable at death rates as the donor died within seven years. Since he died within three years the gifts are taxable in full without the benefit of taper relief. The two inter vivos gifts to John will both fall within the nil rate band but there will be tax due on the gift to Aunt Agatha Brown. IHT will be calculated on the value of the house at the date of the gift and not on its higher value at the donor's death. Aunt Agatha is primarily responsible for the tax due and since she has sold the house the instalment option is not available to her. If Aunt Agatha fails to pay the tax, the Revenue may hold John liable as the deceased's executor if the tax is still unpaid 12 months after the death. He may not apply for a certificate of discharge from IHT that may be payable on the PET before the end of two years from the date of death. If John does pay the IHT due there is no statutory right to recover this amount from Aunt Agatha and it is doubtful that such a right exists under the general law. Thus, John must be aware of this potential liability to IHT. Interest will start to run from six months after the end of the month of death.

There will also be IHT due on the ending of William's interest in possession in the trust created by his wife. The primary responsibility for this tax falls on the trustee who is John. The value of the trust fund will be included as part of William's estate for the purpose of calculating the tax due. The tax need not be paid on delivery of the IHT form.

d) There will be a substantial tax bill on this estate. The first source John is likely to look to is the insurance policy which is written in trust for John. The proceeds are not part of William's estate for IHT purposes and as the trustee of the policy John will be able to obtain payment before a grant of probate is issued. He will need to send the death certificate to the company. This will provide sufficient funds to pay the tax due on delivery of the account if the instalment option is exercised in all cases.

Otherwise the Midland Bank might be willing to release the money in William's current account for payment of IHT in return for the appropriate undertakings and John could raise a loan to pay IHT. The interest on such a loan would qualify for income tax relief for 12 months. Since John is the sole trustee as well as the remainderman of the trust, he could utilise the assets in the trust which are in the form of cash capital or easily realisable Stock Exchange investments. As executor of the will, John has authority to act from the date of death and he could sell William's car before obtaining a grant of probate to raise money to pay the IHT due.

In this case the obvious source of funds is the proceeds of the insurance policy. These can be obtained without waiting for a grant of probate and there should be no difficulty in obtaining the money in time to pay the IHT due on delivery of the account and avoid any interest being charged. John should exercise the instalment option in full. He may wish to pay the tax due on the land in full since interest will be charged on the full amount outstanding and the next obvious source is the trust since John as trustee (and beneficiary) can realise these assets without waiting for a grant of probate. It does not seem necessary in this case to need to go to the trouble of persuading the bank to release the money in the current account before a grant is obtained or the expense of borrowing. John could sell the car but he may possibly intend to keep this for himself.

Inland Revenue
Inheritance Tax*

Inland Revenue Account

- For use where the deceased died on or after 18 March 1986 domiciled in the United Kingdom
- Please see IHT 210 for instructions on how to complete this form

* *Capital Transfer Tax in the case of a death before 25 July 1986*

For Official Use

Your reference: ST

Your telephone number: (info requ'd)

Name and address of solicitors ø
WYZ
South House
Brampton
Cleveland
Postcode requ'd

ø All communications concerning Inheritance Tax will be sent to the Solicitors unless the executors or administrators request otherwise.

In the High Court of Justice Family Division (Probate)

The Newcastle District **Registry**

In the estate of WILLIAM SHAW

Date of Grant

Please use CAPITAL letters

Surname	SHAW	Date of birth	20 10 1928
Title and Forenames	MR. WILLIAM	Date of death	30 11 1988

Marital Status *Please tick as appropriate*

Married ☐ Single ☐ Divorced ☐ Widowed ☑

Last usual address

3, BROADWAY
BRAMPTON
CLEVELAND

Postcode requ'd

Surviving Relatives

Husband ☐ Wife ☐ Child~~(ren)~~ ☑ Parent(s) ☐

Domicile

England and Wales ☑ Scotland ☐ N.Ireland ☐

Occupation COMPANY DIRECTOR

Please state the Tax District at which the tax affairs of the deceased were handled		Tax District Reference

Please give the names and permanent addresses of the executors or intending administrators:

JOHN SHAW 32, TYNE STREET DURHAM Postcode requ'd	Postcode
Postcode	Postcode

IHT200

1

Declaration

1. I/~~We~~ desire to obtain a grant of PROBATE of the aforenamed deceased.

2. To the best of my/~~our~~ knowledge and belief all the statements and particulars furnished in this account and its accompanying schedules are true and complete.

Delete paragraph if inappropriate

3. ~~I/We have made the fullest enquiries that are reasonably practicable in the circumstances but have not been able to ascertain the exact value of the property referred to in Exhibit to section . So far as the value can now be estimated, it is stated in section . I/We undertake, as soon as the value is ascertained, to deliver a further account, and to pay both any additional tax payable for which I/We may be liable, and any further tax payable, for which I/We may be liable on the other property mentioned in this account.~~

**Delete what is inappropriate*

4. So far as the tax on the property disclosed in sections 1B, 2B and 3 may be paid by instalments, I/We elect to pay/not to pay* by instalments as indicated in these sections.

Signed by the above-named (John Shaw)

date

Signed by the above-named

date

Signed by the above-named

Warning

An executor or intending administrator who fails to make the fullest enquiries that are reasonably practicable in the circumstances may be liable to penalties.

He or she may be liable to penalties or prosecution if he or she fails to disclose in Section 1A, 1B, 2A, 2B and 3

date

Signed by the above-named

date

(as appropriate) and in his or her answers to the questions on page 3 and at the foot of page 9 all the property to the best of his or her knowledge and belief in respect of which tax may be payable on the death of the deceased.

Transfers of value which need not be reported are

a. gifts or other transfers of value made to the deceased's spouse unless at the time of transfer the deceased was domiciled in the United Kingdom and the spouse was not

b. gifts of money not exceeding £3,000 in any one year, where the executors or intending administrators are satisfied that they are wholly exempt as normal gifts out of income

c. outright gifts to one individual which are clearly exempt as not exceeding £250 in any one year (to 5 April): (for gifts before 6 April 1980 the exemption is restricted to £100 in any one year)

d. other gifts of money, or of shares or securities quoted on the Stock Exchange, where these, together with any other gifts not within (b) or (c) above, do not in total exceed the exemption for gifts of £3,000 in any one year (to 5 April)

2

- Any property mentioned on this page which is subject to Inheritance Tax, whether or nor tax is actually payable, **must** also be included in sections 1A, 1B, 2A, 2B, or 3 of this account as appropriate. If it is claimed that the property is not subject to Inheritance Tax, reasons should be given.
- Even if a full report has been made or any other information relevant to the answers to any of the questions below has been given to an Inland Revenue Office, affirmative answers must nonetheless be given to the appropriate questions. Please also identify the office and quote any relevant official reference.
- Where necessary schedules may be attached.

1. Gifts etc.

For official use only

Please tick yes or no

Did the deceased, within 7 years of his/her death	yes	no
• make any gift, settlement or other transfer of value other than a transfer mentioned in the notes on page 2.	[x]	[ ]
• make any disposition for the maintenance of a relative	[ ]	[x]
• pay any premium on a policy of life assurance not included in Section 1 of this form?	[x]	[ ]
Did the deceased at any time on or after 18 March 1986 dispose of any property by way of gift where either		
• possession and enjoyment of the property was not bona fide assumed by the donee, or	[ ]	[ ]
• the property was not enjoyed to the entire exclusion of the donor and of any benefit to him/her by contract or otherwise?	[ ]	[ ]

Insurance policy effected 1983 written in trust for JS absolutely JS – trustee. Premiums paid – £2500 pa. Sums payable – £100,000.

If the reply to any of the questions above is "yes", please give full particulars including dates, details of any property affected and the names and addresses of the other parties concerned, on a separate sheet of paper. *(info req'd)*

2. Settled property

	yes	no
• Was the deceased, at the time of his/her death, entitled to a life interest, annuity or other interest in possession in settled property whether as beneficiary under the settlement or otherwise?	[x]	[ ]

- Did the deceased cease to be entitled to any such interest in settled property within 7 years of his/her death? ☐ ☑ Life tenant of trust created by will of Wife. Died 1/7/86.

If the reply to either question is "yes", please give full particulars of the title (including, in the case of a Will/intestacy, the name and date of death of the testator/intestate and date and place of grant). Where the interest was under a settlement and no previous report has been made, kindly forward a copy of the settlement.

3. Nominations

Did the deceased in his lifetime nominate any Savings Bank Account, Savings Certificates or other assets in favour of any person? ☐ ☑

If you have answered "yes", please give full particulars in section 2 on page 8.

4. Joint property

Was the deceased joint owner of any property of any description or did he/she hold any money on a joint account (apart from property or money of which he/she was merely a trustee)? ☐ ☑

If you have answered "yes" please give the following details on a separate sheet of paper

- the date when the joint ownership began (or the date of opening the joint account)
- The name(s) of the other joint owner(s)
- By whom and from what source the joint property was provided and, if it or its purchase price was contributed by one or more of the joint owners, the extent ot the contribution made by each
- how the income (if any) was dealt with and enjoyed
- whether the deceased's interest passed under his/her will or intestacy or by survivorship.

3

Section 1

A schedule of all the property of the deceased within the United Kingdom to which the deceased was beneficially entitled and **in respect of which the grant is made,** excluding property over which the deceased had and exercised by will a general power of appointment. The appointed property should be included in Section 3. Property gifted by the deceased subject to a reservation retained by the deceased should also be included in Section 3 rather than here.

Section 1A Property without the Instalment Option

For official use only

	Gross value at date of death*
Stocks, shares, debentures and other securities as set out in CAP 40:	
• **Quoted** in the Stock Exchange daily official list except so far as included in Section 1B	
• **Others,** except so far as included in Section 1B Shares in P Ltd	3,000
National Savings Certificates and interest to the date of death	
Uncashed dividents and **interest received, dividends declared,** and **interest accrued due,** in respect of the above investments, to the date of death, as statement annexed	
Cash at the bank:	
• On current account and interest (if any) to the date of death at Midland Bank, Brampton	30,000
• On deposit and interest to the date of death at	
Cash (other than cash at banks)	

Money at a National or Trustee Savings Bank and **interest** to the date of death, as statement annexed

Money out on Mortgage, and **interest** to the date of death, as statement annexed

Money with a building society, co-operative or friendly society, and **interest** to the date of death, as statement annexed

Money out on promissary notes, bonds and other securities, and **interest** to the date of death, as statement annexed

Other debts due to the deceased and **interest** to the date of death, except book debts included in Section 1B, as statement annexed

Unpaid purchase money of real and leasehold property contracted in the lifetime of the deceased to be sold, as statement annexed

Rents of the deceased's own real and leasehold property to the date of death

Apportionment of the rents of the deceased's real and leasehold property to the date of death

Income accrued due, but not received before the death, arising from real and personal property, in which the deceased had a life or other limited interest, viz:-

Apportionment of Income from that source to the date of death

Any other income, apportioned where necessary, to which the deceased was entitled at his death (eg pensions, annuities, director's fees, etc) as statement annexed

Policies of insurance and bonuses (if any) thereon, on the life of the deceased, as statement annexed

Saleable value of policies of insurance and bonuses (if any) not payable on the death of the deceased, as statement annexed

** All claims for exemptions or reliefs should be made in the Summary on page 10*

To be carried forward 33,000

4

Section 1A **Continued**

For official use only

Gross value at date of death*

Brought forward 33,000

Household and personal goods, including pictures, china, linen, clothes, books plate, jewels, motor cars, boats, etc.

Sold, realised gross £

Unsold, estimated £ 30,000 — 30,000

(Private car – £28,000; miscellaneous house contents – £2,000)

The deceased's interest expectant upon death of

aged years, under the will/intestacy of

who died on the
or under a settlement dated the
and made between

(setting out the parties to the deed), in the property set out in the statement annexed, of which fund the present trustees are

Tick as appropriate

Was the interest at any time acquired for value whether by the deceased or a predecessor in title? Yes ☐ No ☐

Income tax payable

Other personal property not comprised under the preceding heads
Please give details

Gross property not subject to the instalment option to be carried to page 6 and to the Probate Summary on page 12

63,000

* *All claims for exemptions or reliefs should be made in the Summary on page 10*

Section 1A continued

Schedule of liabilities and funeral expenses. Particulars of the funeral expenses of the deceased and the liabilities due and owing from him at the time of his death to persons resident within the United Kingdom or to persons resident out of the United Kingdom but contracted to be paid in the United Kingdom, or charged on property situated within the United Kingdom (other than liabilities deducted in Section 1B or section 2 under footnote (b) on page 8).

Name and address of creditor	Description of liability	Amount	For official use only
Inland Revenue (address requ'd)	Estimated tax due to date of death	9,000	

Funeral expenses

C + Co. (address requ'd)	1,000
Total to be carried to the Summary below and to the Probate Summary on page 12	10,000

Summary

Gross property (from page 5) not subject to the instalment option	63,000
Less total of liabilities and funeral expenses from above	10,000
Net property in the United Kingdom not subject to the instalment option to be carried to page 11 (Section 1A, net total before relief(s)	53,000

Section 4 on page 9 must be completed in respect of all liabilities listed in the above schedule.

Section 1B **Property with the Instalment Option**

For official use only

Tick as appropriate

- Is the tax on this property to be paid on delivery of this account? Yes ☐ No ☐
- Is payment to be made in yearly instalments? Yes ☐ No ☐

info required

	Value at date of death
Land etc. owned by the deceased in the United Kingdom (not being settled land) whether or not subject to a trust for sale as described on Cap 37 annexed. 3 Broadway, Brampton	50,000
Shaw Farm, nr Brampton	400,000
Business interests	
• Net value of deceased's interest in the business(es), as statement or balance sheet annexed.	
• Net value of deceased's interest as partner in the firm of ________ as statement or balance sheet annexed	
Stocks, shares, debentures and other securities, as set out on Cap 40.	
• Shares or securities etc within Section 228(1) (a) Inheritance Tax Act 1984 which gave the deceased control of the company immediately before his death *see Section 269 Inheritance Tax Act 1984.* Shares in F Ltd	100,000
• Other unquoted shares or securities etc. within Section 228(1) (b) or (c) or (d) Inheritance Tax Act 1984 (all other unquoted shares to be included in Section 1A).	

Value of property within the instalment option to be carried to the Probate Summary on Page 12. — 550,000

Liabilities charged at the date of the deceased's death on the property included above other than those already taken into account above

Particulars of liability	**Property on which charged**	**Amount**

Total liabilities to be carried to the Probate Summary on page 12.

Value of property with the instalment option less liabilities to be carried to page 11 (Section 1B, net total before reliefs). — 550,000

* *All claims for exemptions and reliefs should be made in the Summary on page 10.*

Section 4 on page 9 must be completed in respect of all liabilities listed above

Section 2

All other property on which the personal representatives are liable to pay the tax (or would be liable if any tax were payable) including:-

- all nominated property and property passing by survivorship
- all property situated outside the UK

Section 2A - Property without the Instalment Option

For official use only

Particulars of the property, local situation and details of disposition if nominated or in joint names	**Value at date of death**
Gross Value	

Liabilities[+] **in respect of the property above**

Name and Address of Creditor	**Description of liability**	**Amount**
	Total liabilities	

Net value to be carried to page 11 (Section 2A, net total before reliefs)

Section 2B - Property with the Instalment Option

Tick as appropriate

- Is the tax on this property to be paid on delivery of this account? ☐ Yes ☐ No
- Is payment to be made by yearly instalments? ☐ Yes ☐ No

Particulars of the property, local situation and details of disposition if nominated or in joint names	**Value at date of death**
Gross Value	

Liabilities* **In respect of the property above**

Name and Address of Creditor	**Description of Liability**	**Amount**
	Total liabilities	

Net value to be carried to page 11 (Section 2B, net total before reliefs)	

* *All claims for exemptions or reliefs should be made in the Summary on page 10*

+ *Liabilities* *(a) due from the deceased at the time of his death to persons resident outside the United Kingdom (other than liabilities contracted to be paid in the United Kingdom, or charged on property within the United Kingdom which have been deducted in Sections 1A and 1B) or*
(b) (so far as not included in (a) charged upon incurred in connection with or otherwise affecting the property included in this Section

Section 4 on page 9 must be completed in respect of all liabilities listed above.

8

Section 3

Any other property in the UK and elsewhere in which the deceased had or is treated as having had a beneficial interest in possession immediately before his death including:-

- property over which the deceased had and exercised by will a general power of appointment.
- property outside the UK comprised in a settlement made by a UK domiciled person.
- property gifted by the deceased subject to a reservation retained by the deceased.

Part 1 Property on which tax is elected to be paid on delivery of this account should be listed below and headed "Part 1"

- Is the tax on any property with the Instalment Option to be paid by yearly instalments? *Tick as appropriate*

  ☐ Yes ☐ No

- Separate net totals for Part 1 (property without the instalment option) and Part 1 (property with the instalment option) should be carried to page 11 (Sections 1a (non-instalment option property) and 1b (instalment option property) net totals before reliefs).

Part 2 Property on which tax is not to be paid on delivery of this account should be listed below and headed "Part 2" and its net value carried to page 11 (Section 1c, net total before reliefs).

Separate consecutive numbering for part 1 and part 2	Particulars of the property	Net value at date of death *		For official use only
		Property without the instalment option £	Property with the instalment option £	
Part 2	Elizabeth Shaw Will Trust - ref: F678/1986 Deceased was life tenant under trust created by will of ES who died 1/7/86. The present trustee is John Shaw.			

	Assets Stock Exchange Investments Cash, capital: net of accrued liabilities	65,000 35,000		

* *All claims for exemptions or reliefs should be made in the Summary on page 10*

Section 4

Deductions of liabilities listed in this account

Tick as appropriate

Yes ☐ No ☐

In the case of any liability for which a deduction has been taken in either section 1A, 1B, 2A, 2B or 3 of this account did the consideration for any such debt or incumbrance incurred or created on or after 18 March 1986 consist of property derived from the deceased or was the consideration given by any person who was at any time entitled to, or amongst whose resources there was at any time included any property derived from the deceased?

If "Yes", please give full particulars, including the liabilities in question, the consideration given and the derivation of that consideration from the deceased.

Please attach schedules as necessary.

9

Summary of exemptions and reliefs against capital

- please see instruction booklet IHT 210 as to how this page should be completed
- Schedules should be attached as necessary

Property in respect of which exemption or relief is claimed. The description should not be more detailed than is necessary to identify the property	Nature of exemption or relief claimed	Net value of property £	Amounts exemption or relief claimed £	For official use only
Property included in Section 1A				
£20,000	s23 IHTA '84 to Laing Art Gallery (if charity)	20,000	20,000	
Shares in P Ltd	Business property relief s104	3000	900 30%	
Total of exemptions and reliefs Section 1A to be carried to page 11 (reliefs column)				
Property included in Section 1B				
65% shareholding in F Ltd 6500 shares of £1	s104 IHTA '84 business property relief	100 000	50,000	

Shaw Farm, nr. Brampton	s115 - agricultural property relief	400,000	200,000

Total of exemptions and reliefs Section 1B to be carried to page 11 (reliefs column) 270,400

Property included in other sections - state and show separately which section (sections 2A and B and 3 (Part 1) and 3 (Part 2)
A separate total of exemptions and reliefs for each of these sections should be carried to page 11 (reliefs column)

10

PART THREE
TAX

9 TAX CONSIDERATIONS

9.1 Introduction

Almost every aspect of wills, probate and administration involves tax considerations. Before death, a testator must be advised on the tax consequences of lifetime and testamentary dispositions; after death the PRs must be advised on the tax liability of the estate and of themselves during the administration. The most important type of taxation for these purposes will be inheritance tax (IHT), although both capital gains tax (CGT) and income tax require some consideration.

9.2 Key points

a) *Inheritance tax (IHT)*

IHT is payable on chargeable transfer. A chargeable transfer is a transfer of value by an individual which is not exempt. On death, the deceased is treated as having made a transfer of value immediately before death equal to the value of his estate at that time.

i) Lifetime transfers

PETs

If the transferor makes an outright gift to another, this transfer will be a potentially exempt transfer (PET). No IHT will be charged at the time of the transfer; the transfer will only become chargeable if the transferor dies within seven years.

Chargeable transfers

If the transfer is not an outright gift, but involves, for example, a discretionary trust, then it will be a chargeable transfer and liable to IHT. The transfer must be cumulated with similar transfers within the previous seven years in order to establish the appropriate rate of IHT (see post). At the time of the transfer, IHT is payable at half of the appropriate rate. If the transferor dies within seven years, further IHT will then become payable. The value transferred is the loss to transferor's estate, and this will include the IHT to be paid at the time. Thus, the amount transferred must be grossed-up at the rate of IHT payable at that time in order to determine the IHT payable.

ii) The estate

The estate is all of the property to which the deceased was beneficially entitled.

The estate includes, inter alia:

- life policies on the deceased's life where the deceased retains beneficial ownership;
- the value of a life policy in the deceased's name on the life of another;
- joint property;
- lump sums payable as of right to the deceased's PRs or to nominees under a pension scheme;
- partnership property;
- settled property in which the deceased had a life interest;
- nominated property;
- DMCs;
- property subject to a reservation.

The estate does not include, inter alia:

- life policies on the deceased's life which create a trust in favour of a third party;
- funds payable at trustees' discretion from the deceased's pension scheme;
- excluded property:

  foreign property and some UK property held by a person domiciled outside the UK; *and*

  reversionary interests which have not yet fallen into possession unless it was acquired for valuable consideration or the deceased (or his spouse) was also the settlor.

iii) Calculating IHT

The estate is cumulated with lifetime chargeable transfers and PETs made within the previous seven years. IHT is charged on the total as follows:

- Up to £128,000 - 0 per cent
- Over £128,000 - 40 per cent

Credit is given for IHT which has already been paid on lifetime chargeable transfers.

Tapering relief is available in respect of lifetime chargeable transfers and PETs, dependant on when the transfer was made.

IHT is charged at the following percentage of 40 per cent:

- Transfer made within three years of death - 100 per cent
- Between three and four years - 80 per cent

- Between four and five years - 60 per cent
- Between five and six years - 40 per cent
- Between six and seven years - 20 per cent

Where it is necessary to calculate the IHT attributable to a particular asset, the relevant rate is the rate of IHT attributable to the estate as a whole (the estate rate).

$$\text{Estate rate} = \left[\frac{\text{total tax payable} \times 100}{\text{chargeable estate}} \right] \text{ per cent}$$

iv) Exemptions and reliefs

Exemptions re: lifetime transfers

- The first £3,000 of transfers each year is exempt. (This exemption can be carried forward to the following year.)
- Transfers of up to £250 to each donee each year are exempt.
- If the transfer is normal expenditure out of income, it is exempt.
- Gifts in consideration of marriage are exempt as follows:

  Up to £5,000 from a parent;

  Up to £2,500 from a remoter ancestor or a party to the marriage;

  Up to £1,000 in all other cases.
- Funds spent on family maintenance are exempt.

Exemptions re: lifetime transfers and the estate

- Transfers between spouses.
- Gifts to charities, political parties or for national purposes are exempt.
- Gifts of works of art and historic buildings, provided they are made available for scholars to see.

Reliefs re: lifetime transfers and the estate

- Business property

  The value transferred is reduced by:

  50 per cent on - a business or a partnership share

  - shares or securities if the transferor had control of the company immediately before the transfer.
  - other shares when the minority holding is between 25 per cent and 50 per cent.

30 per cent on	-	other shares.
	-	land or buildings or machinery or plant which immediately before the transfer were used wholly or mainly for the business which the transferor controlled (if a company) or in which he was a partner.

All of the business property mentioned above must have been owned by the transferor for two years before the transfer.

Lifetime chargeable transfers and PETs only qualify at death if at that time the transferee still owns the original or replacement property. (This also applies to agricultural property below.)

- Agricultural property

  If the transferor occupied the property for two years before the transfer or owned it for seven years prior to the transfer (and if it was farmed during the seven-year period), its agricultural value will be reduced by:

  50 per cent - if the transferor was a working farmer.

  30 per cent - if not.

  (Agricultural value is the value of the property if it were subject to a covenant prohibiting any other use.)

- Quick succession relief (only available on death)

  Where a person dies within five years of a chargeable transfer being made to him, the IHT payable on his death on the transfer will be reduced by the following per cent of IHT charged on the previous transfer to him:

if the transfer was made within one year of death	-	100 per cent
between one and two years	-	80 per cent
between two and three years	-	60 per cent
between three and four years	-	40 per cent
between four and five years	-	20 per cent

- Woodlands (only available on death)

  The PRs can elect within two years of death to exclude from the estate the value of growing timber on land comprised in the estate. The deceased must either have been beneficially entitled to land for five years before death or have acquired it for valuable consideration. The IHT is only deferred and becomes payable on a later sale or inter vivos gift.

v) Valuation of the estate

Property is generally valued at the price it might reasonably be expected to fetch if sold on the open market at the moment before death.

Relevant considerations

The following changes in value caused by death will be taken into account.

- If the deceased was the managing director and a major shareholder of a private company and his death causes a decrease in the value of the shares the lower value will be the value for IHT purposes.
- If the deceased has a life insurance policy on his own life and for his own benefit, and its surrender value is less than its value on death, the higher value will be the value for IHT purposes.

Quoted stocks and shares will be valued at 1/4 np from its lower to its higher quoted price.

Liabilities of the deceased

Liabilities of the deceased are deducted when valuing the estate, to the extent that such liabilities were incurred for valuable consideration or were imposed by law or are reasonable funeral expenses.

Where the liability is an encumbrance on a particular asset, it will reduce the value of that asset.

Securities and land

Where certain securities are sold within one year after death and the aggregate sale price of all such securities are less than their value at death, the loss on sale may be deducted from the value of securities on death.

A similar relief applies to land sold within three years after death.

If this IHT loss relief is claimed, the sale price becomes the probate value for IHT purposes and the loss can not also be used as a loss for CGT purposes.

Income accrued prior to death

Income payable before death forms part of the estate even if it relates to the period after death.

Income payable after death relating to a period crossing death is apportioned on a day-to-day basis and that relating to the period prior to death forms part of the estate.

vi) Law of Property Act 1925 s184 and survivorship clauses

Section 184

Under s184 if two or more persons die in circumstances where it is impossible to determine the order of death, the elder is deemed to die first for the purposes of succession.

However, for IHT purposes, they are deemed to die at the same instant. Thus, if the elder left property to the younger it is taxed as part of the elder's estate and not as part of the younger's estate.

Survivorship clauses

Advantages:

- Prevents 'bunching of estates' which may save tax:

  With non-spouse beneficiaries - the clause prevents a second charge to IHT if the beneficiary dies within the survivorship period.

  With spouse beneficiaries - if the clause is included and the spouse dies within the period, IHT is payable on the death of the first spouse to die and not on the second.

- Testator retains control over the property.

Disadvantages:

- It may increase tax liability.
- It delays the distribution of the estate.

A survivorship clause will generally reap tax benefits unless one spouse has used their nil rate band in lifetime transfers in the previous seven years, and the other spouse's estate is too small to utilise their nil rate band.

vii) IHT liability. Who pays?

The following are concurrently liable to the Revenue for IHT on the deceased's estate:

- PRs - for IHT on the deceased's free estate and on UK settled land which devolves on them.
- Settlement trustees - for IHT on property which was settled immediately before death.
- Any person in whom property is vested after death or who is beneficially entitled to an interest in possession in the property.

The following are concurrently liable for IHT payable as a result of the deceased's death within seven years of a PET or a chargeable transfer:

- The donee of the transfer.
- PRs if tax remains unpaid 12 months from the end of the month of death.

'Free estate' is all property which is not comprised in a settlement immediately before death.

'Settlement' is:

- property held in trust for persons in succession;

- property held in trust for any person subject to a contingency;
- property held by trustees on trust to pay the income to beneficiaries at their discretion;
- property held on trust to accumulate the whole or part of the income.

viii) IHT burden. From whose interest is the IHT taken?

This is generally determined by the will, but if the will is silent:

- IHT on UK property which vests in the PRs and which was not comprised in a settlement immediately before death is a testamentary expense and is payable in accordance with the statutory order: first, undisposed of property; second, residue; then ... (see chapter 7).
- IHT on other property is borne by the beneficiary.

ix) Administration

IHT is due six months after the end of the month of death.

PRs must deliver an account to the Inland Revenue of all the property in the deceased's estate within 12 months of the end of the month of death or within three months of the date when the PRs first began to act, whichever is later. PRs must pay the IHT on the delivery of the account.

Unpaid IHT carries interest as at 9 per cent from the date it is due.

Payment by instalments

A right to pay IHT by ten yearly instalments applies to:

- land;
- shares and securities giving the deceased control;
- unquoted shares or securities (not giving control) if:

  they form a sufficiently large holding; *or*

  the Revenue is satisfied that IHT can not be paid at once without undue hardship; *or*

  IHT payable by instalments is at least 20 per cent of IHT payable on the deceased's estate as a whole;
- a business or an interest in a business;
- timber.

If the option is exercised, the first instalment falls due six months after the end of the month of death.

Interest is payable on outstanding instalments except of agricultural land or shares or securities in a company whose business does not consist of investment. If the instalment-option property is sold, the outstanding instalments must be paid immediately.

Inland Revenue charge

A charge for unpaid tax attaches to any property on which tax is chargeable except personal property (including leaseholds and property held as tenants in common). Any disposition of the property will be subject to the charge.

A purchase for valuable consideration without notice takes free of the charge, and the charge attaches to the proceeds of sale.

Certificate of discharge

This will be given when all tax has been paid, and discharges all persons from any further claim to IHT and extinguishes any charges. It should be applied for by the PRs before distributing the estate.

b) *Capital gains tax (CGT)*

i) PRs

On death, there is no deemed disposal for CGT purposes but the PRs (and subsequently the beneficiaries) are deemed to acquire the estate at market value. Transfers to beneficiaries are not deemed disposals.

Gains on other disposals by the PRs are chargeable as at 25 per cent. PRs have a £5,000 annual exemption for the tax year of death and for the following two tax years.

Losses made by the PRs can be set off against their own gains but they can not pass their losses to the beneficiaries to use, nor can they use the losses made by the deceased before death.

ii) The deceased

If CGT on disposals before death have not been paid, it becomes a debt of the estate.

Losses made by the deceased in the tax year of death must first be set against the gains of the deceased in the tax year of death and then against the gains in the three preceding tax years, taking the later years first.

c) *Income tax*

i) Tax liability of the deceased

PRs are liable for income tax payable by the deceased on income before death.

Income due before death is income of the deceased; income due after death is income of the estate (even if it relates to the period before death).

The deceased has a full personal allowance in the year of death.

ii) Liability to tax on income during the administration period

Liability of the PRs

PRs are liable to income tax at the basic rate on all the income of the estate. No personal reliefs are available, but charges can be deducted. (Charges include the interest paid by PRs on a loan to pay IHT on personal property which vests them. This relief is available for one year.)

If taxed income is paid to the beneficiaries, they will be given a tax deduction certificate to show how much tax was paid.

Liability of the beneficiaries

- Residuary beneficiaries:

  Life tenant of the residue

  A life tenant receives income net of basic rate tax. At the end of the administration period, the net amounts are spread evenly over the period on a day-to-day basis and are grossed-up at basic rate for each tax year. The adjusted income will already have borne tax. A credit will be given for this and extra tax will be paid by the beneficiary or reclaimed by him as appropriate.

  Residuary beneficiary who is absolutely entitled

  Sums paid to the residuary beneficiary during the administration period in any one tax year are deemed to be income up to the actual amount of net residuary income generated. Any extra sums are treated as capital.

  At the end of the administration period, the initial assessments are adjusted so that the beneficiary is deemed to receive the full net residuary income in each tax year.

- Other beneficiaries:

  General and pecuniary gifts

  Any interest received forms part of the beneficiary's statutory income.

  Specific gifts

  Income from the property from the date of death becomes part of the beneficiary's statutory income as it arises.

  Before the PRs have assented to the vesting of the property in the beneficiary, the income is taxed as the beneficiary's income and is paid by the PRs.

  On vesting, the net accrued income and a tax deduction certificate is handed over to the beneficiary.

  After vesting, the beneficiary is liable for income tax on the income.

d) *Post-death variations*

Gifts under a will or under intestacy can be varied by those entitled to them.

i) Disclaimer

A beneficiary can disclaim his entitlement provided that:

- he refuses the whole of the entitlement; *and*
- no benefit has been accepted from the property.

The result is that the property results to the deceased's estate and then passes as part of the residue or under the intestacy rules. The original beneficiary has no control over the destination of the property.

If the disclaimer is made in writing within two years of death, it will not be treated as a transfer of value for IHT purposes or as a disposal for CGT purposes. Stamp duty will not be payable.

It will be taxed as if the deceased had left the property to the person next entitled.

ii) Variation

A beneficiary can take the gift and then make an inter vivos gift of all or part of the property to anyone he wants to benefit, by directing the PRs to transfer the property to someone else. This can be done even if the original beneficiary has accepted some benefit of the property.

If the variation is made in writing within two years of death, it will not be treated as a transfer of value or as a disposal provided the beneficiary so elects by giving written notice to the Revenue within six months of the variation.

If the election is made the gift will be taxed as if the deceased had left the property to the person who benefits under the variation.

If further IHT becomes payable because of the variation, the PRs must join in the election. (They cannot refuse to do so if they have sufficient funds available to meet the additional liability.)

e) *Settlements*

i) Settlements fall broadly into three categories:

Settlement with an interest in possession - an interest in possession is an interest which gives a present right to the present enjoyment of property (ie an immediate right to receive income or to use and enjoy the property).

Settlement without an interest in possession

Accumulation and Maintenance (A & M) Settlement - if Trustee Act 1925 s31 has not been excluded, a settlement will be an A & M settlement if:

- beneficiaries will become entitled to the settled property (or to an interest in possession) on or before an age not exceeding 25 (if no age is specified, it will be 18); *and*
- no interest in possession subsists in the settled property (the income being accrued in so far as it is not applied for the maintenance, education or benefit of the beneficiary); *and*
- either:

  no more than 25 years have elapsed since the creation of the settlement; *or*

  all the beneficiaries are grandchildren of a common grandparent.

ii) IHT

Settlement with interest in possession

Its creation is a transfer of value. (If it is a lifetime transfer, it is a PET.)

If the beneficiary disposes of his interest before death, he is treated as making a transfer of value equal to the value of the settled property and this will be a PET. When the beneficiary becomes entitled to the property, there is no charge to IHT.

Settlement without an interest in possession

Its creation is a chargeable transfer. After creation:

- a periodic charge to IHT occurs on the tenth anniversary of the creation of the settlement as at 30 per cent of the hypothetical lifetime rate.
- a proportionate periodic charge occurs when the property leaves the settlement or when the beneficiary acquires an interest in possession.

A & M settlement

Its creation is a transfer of value. (If it is a lifetime transfer, it is a PET.)

After creation, there is no periodic or proportionate periodic charge.

iii) CGT

Settlement with an interest in possession

When the beneficiary becomes entitled to the capital, there is a deemed disposal at market value.

Settlement without an interest in possession

CGT is not relevant.

A & M settlement

If the interest is contingent, there will be a disposal of market value when the beneficiary becomes absolutely entitled to the capital.

iv) Income tax

Settlement with an interest in possession

There is a vested interest in income. The trustees are liable for basic rate tax on the gross amount of all trust income.

Settlement without an interest in possession

There is a contingent interest in income. The trustees are liable for basic rate tax plus an additional amount (10 per cent) on the gross amount of trust income.

A & M settlement

Income tax liability depends on whether the interest is vested or contingent (see above).

Trustees can set management expenses (grossed up at basic rate tax) against gross income for the purpose of ascertaining additional rate liability but not in calculating basic rate liability.

10 QUESTIONS (TAX)

Taxation is examined, and suggested solutions are provided, in the questions and solutions in Part One (Pre-Death) and Part Two (Post-Death).

The relevant parts of questions are as follows:

Chapter 4	question 1(a)(i)
	question 2(b)
	question 3(a)(ii) and (iv)
	question 3(b)
	question 4(b)
	question 4(c)
	question 4(d)
	question 5(a)
	question 5(b)
	question 6(a)
Chapter 8	question 1(b)
	question 1(c)
	question 2(a)
	question 3(d)
	question 3(e)
	question 4(c)
	question 4(d)
	question 4(e)
	question 5(h)
	question 6(a)
	question 6(b)
	question 6(c)
	question 6(d)

HLT GROUP PUBLICATIONS FOR THE LLB EXAMINATIONS

Our publications, written by specialists, are used widely by students at universities, polytechnics and colleges throughout the United Kingdom and overseas.

Textbooks
These are designed as working books to provide students with a valuable framework on which to base their studies. They are updated each year to reflect new developments and changing trends.

Casebooks
These are designed as companion volumes to the Textbooks and incorporate important cases, statutes as appropriate, and other material, together with detailed commentaries.

Revision WorkBooks
For first degree law students, these provide questions and answers for all topics in each law subject. Every topic has sections on key points, recent cases and statutes, further reading etc.

Suggested Solutions
These are available to past London University LLB examination papers and provide the student with an invaluable revision aid and an insight into the techniques essential to examination success.

The books listed below can be ordered through your local bookshops or obtained direct from the publisher using this order form. Telephone, Fax or Telex orders will also be accepted. Quote your Access or Visa card numbers for priority orders. To order direct from the publisher please enter the cost of the titles you require, fill in the despatch details and send it with your remittance to the HLT Group Ltd.

ORDER FORM

LLB PUBLICATIONS	Textbooks		Casebooks		Revision WorkBooks		Sug. Sol. 1984/88		Sug. Sol. 1989	
	Cost £	£	Cost £	£	Cost £	£	Cost £	£	Cost £	£
L01 Criminal Law	12.95		16.95		9.95		14.95		3.95	
L02 Constitutional Law	12.95		16.95		9.95		14.95		3.95	
L03 English Legal System	12.95		14.95				*6.95		3.95	
L04 Law of Contract	12.95		15.95		9.95		14.95		3.95	
L05 Law of Tort	12.95		16.95				14.95		3.95	
L06 Law of Trusts	12.95		16.95		9.95		14.95		3.95	
L07 Land Law	12.95		18.95		9.95		14.95		3.95	
L08 Jurisprudence	14.95				9.95		14.95		3.95	
L09 Administrative Law	15.95		18.95				14.95		3.95	
L10 Law of Evidence	17.95		14.95		9.95		14.95		3.95	
L11 Commercial Law	17.95		18.95		9.95		14.95		3.95	
L13 Pub. Int. Law	16.95		14.95		9.95		14.95		3.95	
L14 Succession	14.95		15.95		9.95		14.95		3.95	
L16 Family Law	14.95		18.95				14.95		3.95	
L17 Company Law	16.95		18.95		9.95		14.95		3.95	
L18 Revenue Law	14.95		18.95		9.95		14.95		3.95	
L20 European Community Law	15.95									

Cut along dashed line

* 1987 and 1988 only

DETAILS FOR DESPATCH OF PUBLICATIONS

Please insert your full name below

Please insert below the style in which you would like correspondence to be addressed to you

TITLE Mr, Miss etc.	INITIALS	SURNAME/FAMILY NAME

Address to which study material is to be sent (please ensure someone will be present to accept delivery of your College Publications.)

POSTAGE & PACKING

You are welcome to purchase study material from the College at 200 Greyhound Road W14 9RY, during normal working hours.

If you wish to order by post this may be done direct from the College. Postal charges are as follows:

UK - all orders over £25 - no charge; orders below £25 - £1.50.

OVERSEAS - all orders are sent by airmail and the charge is £6 for the first item, an additional £4 for the second item and an additional £3 for the third and for every additional item. If ordering *Suggested Solutions 1989 only* add 30% to the charge for the Suggested Solutions ordered.

The College cannot accept responsibility in respect of postal delays or losses in the postal systems.

DESPATCH All cheques must be cleared before material is despatched.

SUMMARY OF ORDER

Date of order: / /

Cost of publications ordered: £

Add: Postage and packing United Kingdom (see above) £

Overseas Air Mail: First item at £6; Second item at £4;

Additional items at £3; Suggested Solutions only: 30%

Total cost of order: £

Please ensure that you enclose a cheque or draft payable to The HLT Group Ltd for the above amount, or charge to ☐ Access ☐ Visa

Card Number

Expiry Date / / Signature ____________________

Your completed form and remittance should be sent to :

The HLT Group Ltd, Despatch Department, 200 Greyhound Road, London W14 9RY.

Telephone: (01) 385 3377 Telex: 266386 Fax: (01) 381 3377.

NOTES

NOTES